CONTENTS

Introduction

PART 1. CRAFTING A SPEECH

CHAPTER. 1

DELIVERING A SPEECH-KNOWING YOUR AUDIENCE   **15**

Defining your objectives   15

Formulating objectives   16

Knowing your audience   16

Key Points from Chapter 1   20

CHAPTER. 2

PUBLIC SPEAKING GENERALLY   **21**

The person and the material   22

The Person   22

Why do we feel nervous?   23

Be prepared!   24

Key Points from Chapter 2   26

CHAPTER.3

RESEARCHING, PLANNING AND WRITING A   **27**
SPEECH
Libraries.   28
Newspapers and magazines   28
The web   28
Radio and television   28
Reference books   26
Planning and writing a speech   29
Definition of the topic   29
Composing the title of a speech   30
Structuring a speech   30
Openings   32
Introduction   33
Closing a speech   33
Key Points from Chapter 3   35

PART. 2 PRESENTATION SKILLS

CHAPTER. 4

PRESENTATION SKILLS   **39**
Personal skills   39
Body Language   39
Vision   40
Developing a style   40

A Straightforward Guide

To

Speech Writing and Presentation

Roland Watson

Straightforward Publishing

Windsor and Maidenhead

9580000200459

Straightforward Guides

© Straightforward Co Ltd 2022

978-1-80236-065-3

Printed by 4edge Ltd www.4edge.co.uk

Series Editor: Roger Sproston
Cover design by BW Studio Derby.

Presentation   42

Use of language   42

Body Language   43

Use of hands   43

Using facial expressions   43

Controlling your movements   44

Dress   45

Attitude   45

Formalities   46

Key Points from Chapter 4   49

CHAPTER. 5

THE USE OF VISUAL AIDS   **51**

Presenting with visual images   53

Tools for the presentation of visual aids   54

Use of an Overhead projector and use of power point 54

Slide projectors   54

Using a video   54

Use of other visual aids   54

Use of colour   55

Working with computers   55

Choosing the right equipment   55

Use of notes and handouts   54

Involving the Audience   56

Key Points from Chapter 5   59

CHAPTER 6

EFFECTIVE DELIVERY- THE VOICE   59

The voice   60

Developing your voice   61

Tone   61

Pitch   61

Volume   62

Clarity   62

Voice pitch   62

Use of silences and pauses: 64

A few useful hints on the use of pauses: 64

Emphasis   65

Voice projection   66

Use of the body   66

The nose   67

Improving posture   67

Training and looking after your voice   68

Key Points from Chapter 6   70

CHAPTER 7

EXERCISES GENERALLY   71

Exercises to help you relax   71

Shoulders   72

Neck   72

Head   72

Concentration   72

Breathing control   73

Breathing in   73

Breathing out   74

The voice generally   75

Key Points from Chapter 7   77

CHAPTER 8

A FEW HINTS ON SETTING   **79**

Choosing the right setting   79

Further tips   80

CHAPTER 9

DEALING WITH NERVES   **83**

Perseverance in the face of fear   84

Fear of public speaking   85

Practical ways of controlling fear   87

General health   88

Key Points from Chapter 9   89

CHAPTER 10.

DELIVERING YOUR PRESENTATION   **91**

The eve of your speech   92

The day   92

Arrival   93

Socializing   93

Dealing with hecklers   94

Question time   95

Finally   95

Key Points from Chapter 10   96

CHAPTER 11

THE ART OF REMOTE PRESENTATIONS   **97**

CHAPTER 12

SUMMARY-SPEECH WRITING AND   **109**
PRESENTATION

Useful Websites and Publications   **113**

APPENDIX 1

Public Speaking Roles and Events

1. Acting as compere   101
2. Acting as Master of Ceremonies   102
3. After Dinner Speaking   104
4. Appeals and Fundraising   110
5. Business Meetings-Informal and Formal   112
6. Chairing a Meeting   117
7. Conference and Conventions   120
8. Debating   123
9. Funerals and Memorials   124
10. Key note Speaking   125
11. Weddings/Civil partnerships   127
12. Opening functions   131
13. Political Speeches   133
14. Radio and Television   136

**

INTRODUCTION

This book is designed for those who wish to gain knowledge of the art of speech writing and also find public speaking and presenting in front of others a nerve-wracking experience. It is written in two parts. The bulk of the book concentrates on actual live public speaking events, in front of audiences, whilst the latter part, namely chapter 11, deals with remote presentations which have grown considerably following the pandemic, using the likes of Zoom and other software packages. Remote presentations require a separate set of skills although there are similarities to live presentation.

This is not a book written for experienced speechwriters or presenters. It is very much a back-to-basics book that deals with the fundamentals of speechwriting and presentations for the beginner. There are books out there that deal with the subject on a different level, such as the political level and these books are outlined in the section outlining useful information.

There are a number of key aspects that are fundamental to the art of speech writing and making presentations. Without a doubt the two most important are the person presenting and the nature of the material. This book concentrates heavily on these areas, offering invaluable advice on the structuring of a speech, invaluable tips on different occasions and also essential advice on personal presentation.

In addition, advice on the use of visual aids and on the nature of the setting in which the public speaker will deliver his or her address is offered and also instruction on making the presentation and audience management.

Overall, this book will benefit those people who are new to the area of speech writing, public speaking and making presentations, whatever the medium. However, it will also benefit those who are more experienced but need a refresher.

There are key points at the end of each chapter that help to reinforce the main areas. In addition to the above, in appendix 1 there is advice on delivering speeches different speeches to suit different occasions.

Effective speech writing and public speaking is an art and a skill and the rewards for those who can become effective writer's and presenters are enormous. It is hoped that this book will go some way to developing the skills and abilities needed.

Roland Watson

**

PART 1

CRAFTING A SPEECH

'A scrupulous writer, in every sentence that he writes, will ask himself at least four questions, thus: What am I trying to say? What words will express it? What image or idiom will make it clearer? Is this image fresh enough to have an effect? And he will probably ask himself two more: Could I put it more shortly? Have I said anything that is unavoidably ugly?

George Orwell

CHAPTER 1

WRITING AND DELIVERING A SPEECH-KNOWING YOUR AUDIENCE

The first thing to consider when accepting an invitation to speak is the nature and type of the function in question and also the type of audience that you will be addressing. This is absolutely essential for anyone who is being called on to deliver a speech.

Following this, you will need to set objectives for yourself and to create a framework for your speech based around those objectives. This is the essential starting point for all speech writing and presenting. Objectives fall into several categories:

- The need to entertain your audience and to warm them to you
- The need to pass on essential information
- The need to fire your audience, to inspire them
- The need to persuade the audience
- The need to open up debate.

Defining your objectives
The main objective is the one you want to achieve in the best of circumstances. *The main or primary objective is the one which is your main concern.*

Therefore, it is essential that you have this key objective at the core of what it is you are formulating. Whether your main objective when delivering a speech is to inform, persuade or entertain, it is essential that you provoke some sort of reaction from your audience. When this happens, you have succeeded in your task. You have fulfilled your purpose as a speaker.

Formulating objectives

You need to consider very carefully the task that you have in hand. Basically, you have to speak to a particular type of audience about a given subject on a particular occasion. Formulate a statement of objectives at this point and write it down succinctly.

Include secondary objectives in addition to primary objectives. It may be your main objective to impart information and inform. However, a secondary objective may be to entertain. At least, if the audience is entertained then you will have achieved something. Essentially, in all speeches, you should aim to entertain. This will leave people with a good feeling and not an empty feeling, a feeling that time has been wasted.

Knowing your audience

There is one main golden rule when speaking in public. Always keep your audience in the forefront of your mind. Always meet the expectation of your audience. The speech must be tailored to suit the needs of the audience and to suit their level. Use language that they will understand.

You will need essential information about your audience. The following should be considered:

- What is the make-up of the audience?
- What is the age group?
- What is their interest in the event?
- What economic group are they from?
- What racial and cultural background are they from?
- Are they attending voluntarily or involuntarily?

Write down what it is that you think your audience are interested in and why they are attending the event at which you will be making a speech. You will then be in a position to decide how your subject and your objectives can marry up with what you think are the interests of the audience.

Audiences can be categorized and profiled in terms of their background and their varying levels of expertise. Some audiences are drawn from a profession and others are non-expert audiences. It very much depends on the occasion. Are you addressing a professional gathering or are you at a social gathering such as a wedding? Each occasion will differ and, even before you can consider writing a speech you must carry out thorough research into the audience and the desired outcomes of what it is you are trying to put across.

Write down what you think your audience's level of expertise is likely to be, and then decide how this will affect your speech.

Every audience has a profile of expertise and its own interests in being at an event. One of the fundamental objectives is to join an audience in its common interest and convey your message in a way that can be understood. The key is to gain the audiences attention and to make them ready to listen to what you have to say. A little later in the book we will be looking at techniques when public speaking. If we examine audience needs a little further, psychologists believe that people nowadays have a number of needs and that they are fundamentally the same in everyone. These are:

- Economic needs
- The need for physical comfort
- The need to be free from worry and anxiety
- The need to explore new ideas
- The need to be free from political oppression.

Each member of an audience has these needs and they expect the speaker to fulfil at least one of the needs or indicate how they may do so. It is essential that you fulfil the audience's expectations if your speech is to be successful.

You should assemble everything that you know about your audience, putting together your perception about their particular interests, their reason for attending and their level of expertise and reason for attending the speech. When you have successfully joined the needs and level of your audience with your stated objectives, then you will have completed the necessary pre-planning work which is vital to the construction of a good and effective speech.

The next stage is to start to construct the speech. However, before we consider this stage, we will explore some of the general concepts and practices of public speaking in a little more depth.

Now read the key points from chapter one.

**

KEY POINTS FROM CHAPTER ONE

- The first thing to consider when accepting an invitation to speak is the nature and type of the function in question and also the type of audience

- Following this consideration, you will need to set objectives for yourself and create a framework for your speech.

- The main objective is the one you want to achieve in the best of circumstances. *The main or primary objective is the one which is your main concern.*

- Whether your main objective when delivering a speech is to inform, persuade or entertain, it is essential that you provoke some sort of reaction from your audience. When this happens, you have succeeded in your task. You have fulfilled your purpose as a speaker.

- There is one main golden rule when speaking in public. Always keep your audience in the forefront of your mind. Always meet the expectation of your audience. The speech must be tailored to suit the needs of the audience and to suit their level. Use language that they will understand.

CHAPTER 2

PUBLIC SPEAKING GENERALLY

Before looking at the crafting of a speech, based on what we have been discussing, we need to look at public speaking generally. It is only when you learn the art of public speaking that you can become an accomplished speaker and, by definition, deliver an effective speech. It is much more than just standing up and talking to others, as you will probably have started to gather.

Public speaking is very much an art and a skill that can be mastered by anyone. It is true to say that some people may be initially better equipped for the role of public speaker than others, by virtue of their own particular personality type. However, the truly effective public speaker learns the craft and applies certain techniques that generally derive from experience.

In this book I will be alluding to the person who has to deliver a speech or present a seminar, rather than the professional teacher. It is the person who is not constantly engaged in addressing groups who will most benefit from what is contained within the book.

The person and the material

There are two vital ingredients in public speaking. The first is very much the person delivering the speech or other material to a group. The second is the nature of the material being delivered.

The Person

For some people, standing in front of an audience, whatever the size, is not a real problem. For others however, the very thought of exposing ones self to a group of people, and being so vulnerable, is a nightmare best avoided.

When trying to put this into context it is important to remember that, when we communicate as part of a group, or simply on a one to one basis with another, then we interact primarily through speech and body language. We are often confident within ourselves because we feel secure in that we are part of a group interacting and that all eyes are not on us alone, at least not for a protracted period.

The situation is very different indeed when we are alone and faced with a group of people, strangers or not, and we have to present material. It means that we have to assume responsibility and take the lead and communicate successfully to others. Nervousness is very often the result when placed in this situation because, until we can make contact with the audience and establish a rapport, we are very much alone and feel vulnerable.

Obviously, there are a number of factors influencing the levels of confidence and differences in attitude between people, such as the nature and type of the person and their background, their past experience, both within the family and in the world of work and numerous other experiences besides. All these will affect a person's ability to become an effective public speaker.

This publication cannot completely erase your nervousness. It cannot change your personality overnight. However, what it can certainly do is to raise your awareness to the root of that feeling in the context of public speaking and to help you become more confident. It can also show you that, whatever your personality type, you can become a successful public speaker by applying certain fundamental techniques.

Why do we feel nervous?

There are a number of reasons why we may feel nervous. You need to question yourself and ask yourself why? Was the sight of so many faces in front of you enough to frighten you and make you lose your self-confidence or are you plagued by the memory of previous mistakes? You need to remember that you change and develop as a person as you gain more experience and that past mistakes do not mean that you will repeat them, Lets face it, most of us will experience nerves in a situation which is stressful to us. This is totally normal and quite often we become anxious and charged with adrenaline which drives us on. When it comes to speaking in public the adrenaline can be positive but excessive nerves are negative and can lead to aggression.

Fundamentally, the key to successful public speaking is the acquisition of confidence coupled with assertiveness which leads to the ability to effectively control a situation. If you are assertive and you know your subject matter you are likely to be confident and in control and less likely to feel nervous.

Be prepared!

Directly related to the above, preparation is everything and to feel confident with your material means that you are half way there already. Although I will be expanding on preparation a little later, there are a few fundamental tips that can help you along.

You should listen to speakers, particularly good speakers as often as possible in order to gain tips. Notice the way that good and effective speakers construct their sentences. Listen for the eloquence. Remember, shorter sentences have a lot more impact and are easier to grasp than long sentences. They also act a discipline for the speaker in that they will prevent him or her from straying off the point. Another very important tip when approaching the day of your presentation is preparing yourself psychologically. Convince yourself that you are looking forward to the speech and that you will do well no matter what. Convey this to your audience as you open your presentation, say that you are glad to be with them and that you hope that this goes well for all. This reinforces a feeling of goodwill and will express itself through your body language and your voice.

Finally, one of the main aides to effective public speaking is *experience* and that only comes through practice so it is essential that you take every opportunity offered you to sharpen your skills in this area.

In the next chapter, I will be concentrating on presentation and style. Fundamental to preparation as a speaker is the ability to relax and focus your mind and body on the task ahead.

Now read the key points from chapter two overleaf.

**

KEY POINTS FROM CHAPTER TWO

- The truly effective public speaker learns the craft and applies certain techniques which generally derive from experience

- There are two vital ingredients in public speaking. The first is the person and the second is the material

- The key to successful public speaking is the acquisition of knowledge coupled with assertiveness which leads to the ability to control and direct a situation

- Listen to effective and successful speakers in order to gain tips

- Prepare yourself psychologically for your speech. Put yourself in a positive frame of mind !

CHAPTER 3

RESEARCHING, PLANNING AND
WRITING A SPEECH

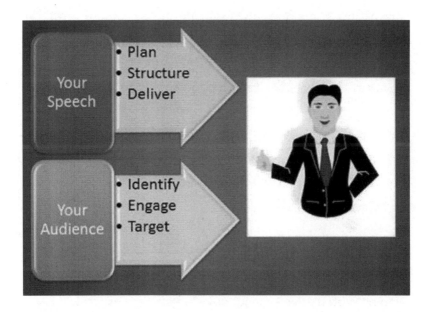

The key to speech preparation is research, thorough research. Take research very seriously because audiences can tell very quickly what level of preparation you are at. You should have developed a little library of information, which again will vary depending on the type of occasions:

Libraries.

The local library should be your starting point. There are many works of reference and in addition libraries are invaluable sources of other information, such as where you can go to develop your subject, any associations that may exist and so on.

Newspapers and magazines

Local and national newspapers are indispensable sources of information. Trade magazines will inform you about a particular profession and other papers, such as free papers, should not be overlooked. You should begin to develop a cuttings file that you can dip into as and when the occasion is right.

The web

Of course, the web is the most convenient place to start any research. Whatever it is that you are researching, information will be available online.

Radio and television

Invaluable again. You should have a notebook waiting by your radio or TV so that you can jot down anything of interest.

Reference books

Good reference books, such as the Guinness book of records and English dictionaries, plus thesaurus are essential for research.

You should file your material and ensure that you have checked the facts before you put together a speech. When and if you use statistics and figures, check them and quote your sources. Make sure that you get it right on the day. Avoid any slander against another. Do not be unprofessional when including facts and figures. Audiences tend to see speakers who indulge in slander as negative and turn away quite quickly.

Planning and writing a speech

When it comes to planning, it is better to have too much material than too little. Ensure that your research is derived from your own personal experience, as much as possible, rather than simply cold hard facts.

A successful speech utilizes relatively small amount of information, which is chosen for its relevance to the audience and for its usefulness in achieving the objectives of the speaker.

Different people have different methods of planning speeches. However, most people will engage in some sort of brainstorming. This involves scribbling down often random thoughts. Brainstorming is useful in that it will produce, after a while, a train of thoughts.

Definition of the topic

Speech writing should be a process of simplification rather than complication. The key is to sort through the mass of material and whittle it down until you have a small, well-defined topic upon which to speak. You will achieve this by writing down words or phrases that cover the subject you want to tackle. Then choose a list of topics that fall into this subject field. Choose the one that most relates to your audiences needs and expectations, and is most likely to enable you to fulfil your objectives. Again, write down a list of sub-topics under your chosen topics heading, and choose one that fits with the context.

Composing the title of a speech

Some organizers require that you let them have a title of your speech in advance. This enables them to include it in the forthcoming program. When you have defined your topic and sorted the information you have, you should then be able to think of a title. Your title should be concise and catchy and it should also make your speech sound interesting. The aim is to get people to come and hear you speak.

Structuring a speech

A good speech is pieced together in a defined structure and contains a number of specific elements. The structure of a speech should comprise the following:

- The opening. This is where the speaker needs to grab the attention of the audience
- Introduction to the subject. This is where the speaker gives an overview of the material to be covered
- The body of the speech. This is where the speaker presents information or arguments

- Close. This is where the speaker draws conclusions from the information already presented and leaves the audience with something to think about.

Although most compositions have a beginning, middle and end speeches can differ somewhat. The most important difference between a speech and other presentations is that a speech is fleeting, it is uttered and then disappears. It is not for a listener of a speech to go back to the beginning if they are not paying attention, at least not during the speech, maybe after with a transcript. The good speechwriter will therefore build in elements so that the audience is kept alert. These elements are:

- Splashes. These are attention grabbers which surprise people and gain their interest right at the beginning

- Appeals. These are where sentences identify the speakers purpose with the needs of the audience

- Links. These are sentences that link one piece of argument to the next in a logical manner

It is easier to write the introduction and main body of your speech before you tackle the opening and the close. You will write a more effective opening and close if you deal with them together at the end of the writing process.

■ Summaries and repetitions. These are useful techniques to ensure that the audience follows the argument and remembers as much as possible after you have stepped out of the limelight. The general rule is: tell them what you are going to tell them; and then tell them what you have told them.

Openings

When a speaker starts, or rises to begin to speak, the audience will appraise him or her on the physical appearance. The second critical moment is when the first words are uttered. Apart from the formal address, the elements to build into the opening are: a splash, an appeal and credentials, followed by a statement of the topic on which you are going to speak.

The splash is a method of grabbing the audience's attention. Choose a splash that is relevant and also topical. Once the audience is paying attention, make them see that your topic is not only interesting, but also relevant to their experience and needs.

Next, prove to the audience that you are someone who has something interesting and worthwhile to say, and that your facts can be relied upon. State your credentials, then give a short sharp simple explanation of what it is that you are going to talk about, and what you hope to achieve by doing so. These last two elements, the statement of your subject and your objectives should be, in effect, a promise to go some way towards fulfilling the audience's needs.

A strong opening should be confident, friendly, short and simple. The speaker who apologizes or who undermines his/herself will lose respect immediately. On the other hand, a long rambling opening will confuse and irritate, boding no good for the rest of the speech.

Introduction

When you have completed the arrangement of the material, you should have a series of headings that lead on from one another logically. Under each of these headings you will have a number of pieces of material to utilize. During the introduction, you need to set out for the audience the main elements of your argument. State each of the headings in the order in which you are going to present them, and explain what they mean. Tell the audience what it is that you are going to tell them.

Closing a speech

It is a fact that most audiences have a very short time span, They are generally attentive at the start of a presentation, but after a few minutes their concentration begins to waver. However, they will usually perk up again towards the end of the speech. The close of the speech is just as important as the opening and it is up to the speaker to make sure that the audience attention is held. The close should be a short summary of all the material that you covered in your presentation, and you should draw any conclusion from the arguments that you have presented. In this way you will repeat the salient points that you wished to put across, and the audience is likely to remember some of what you have said.

Always end on a high note and try to leave the audience with words that sum up your speech. Above all, make sure that you close confidently and that your audience know that the speech is over. Avoid at all cost the pregnant pause or the embarrassed silence.

Now read the key points from chapter three overleaf.

**

KEY POINTS FROM CHAPTER THREE

- The key to speech preparation is thorough research. The type of occasion will determine the level and type of research

- In order to facilitate research you should develop a comprehensive library of information

- When it comes to planning it is better to have too much information than too little

- Speech writing is, above all, a process of simplification. You should sift through all your material until you have a well-defined topic that is not over-laden with information.

PART 2.

PRESENTATION SKILLS

"Look your audience straight in the eyes, and begin to talk as if every one of them owed you money." – Dale Carnegie

"Once you get people laughing, they're listening and you can tell them almost anything." – Herbert Gardner

"The difference between a good speech and a great speech is the energy with which the audience comes to their feet at the end. Is it polite? Is it a chore? Are they standing up because their boss just stood up? No. You want it to come from their socks." – Rob Lowe as Sam Seaborn, *The West Wing*

"Take advantage of every opportunity to practice your communication skills, so that when important occasions arise, you will have the gift, the style, the sharpness, the clarity, and the emotions to affect other people." – Jim Rohn

CHAPTER 4

PRESENTATION SKILLS

Having looked at preparation for speech writing and also structuring a speech, it is now necessary to consider some more specific points connected with presentation of a speech.

Personal skills-Body Language

People have a natural ability to use body language together with speech. Body language emphasises speech and enables us to communicate more effectively with others. It is vitally important when preparing for the role of public speaker to understand the nature of your body language and also to connect this to another all important element-*vision.*

Vision

People tend to take in a lot of information with their eyes and obviously presentations are greatly enhanced by use of visual aids. Together, when presenting to a group of people, as a public speaker, *body language and visual stimuli* are all important. A great amount of thought needs to go into the elements of what it is that you are about to present and the way you intend to convey your message. What you should not do, especially as a novice, is to stand up in front of a group and deliver a presentation off the top of your head. As we have emphasised, you need to carry out thorough research into what it is you are presenting and to whom you are presenting.

Developing a style

Every person engaged in public speaking will have his or her own style. At the one end of the spectrum there are those people who give no thought to what it is they are doing and have no real interest in the audience. For them it is a chore and one which should be gotten over as soon as is possible. Such public speakers can be slow, boring and ineffectual leaving only traces of annoyance in the audiences mind. Here, there is a definite absence of style.

At the other end of the spectrum are those who have given a great deal of thought to what they are doing, given a great deal of thought to their material and have a genuine interest in the audience. Such public speakers will be greatly stimulating and leave a lasting impression and actually convey something of some worth.

It does not matter what the occasion, wedding (best mans speech etc.) seminar, presentation to employers. The principles are the same-that is understanding your material, understand the nature of yourself as you relate to the material and how this will translate into spoken and body language and also how you will use visual aids to enhance the presentation.

Underlying all of this is your *own personal style,* partly which develops from an understanding of the above and partly from understanding of yourself. Some presenters of material recognise their own speed of presentation, i.e. slow, medium or fast and also understand their own body language. Some are more fluent than others, use their hands more etc. Having recognized your own style what you need to do is to adjust your own way of presentation to the specific requirements of the occasion. The key point is to gain attention, get the message across and be stimulating to a degree. Obviously some occasions are more formal than others. You should study the nature of the occasion and give a lot of thought to what is required, i.e. degree of humour, seriousness etc.

All of the above considerations begin to translate themselves into a style that you yourself will begin to recognize and feel comfortable with. Once this occurs you will find that, when presenting, your nerves will begin to melt away and your confidence begins to develop.

Presentation

As this is a book about speech writing, and also presentation, we should now concentrate on the various elements which go to make up a successful presentation to a group. There is not one particular style appropriate to public speaking. Each occasion will merit it's own approach. However, there are a few commonly observed rules.

Use of language

The use of language is a specific medium that must be understood when making a presentation. Obviously. if you are speaking publicly to a group of familiar people who know and understand you, a different approach will be needed and a different form of language, perhaps less formal, utilized than that used in front of a group who are totally unfamiliar.

Nevertheless, using formal but simple language interspersed with funny remarks is undoubtedly one of the best ways to approach any form of audience, friends or not. You should certainly avoid too much detail and do not go overboard with funny comments as this will become tedious. Stick to the subject matter, lightening up the occasion with a few anecdotes and witty comments. It is all about the right blend and pitch.

Body Language

We have briefly discussed body language. It is astounding how much you can tell about people in the street by simply observing their body language. Usually people form an impression about another person within the first five minutes of meeting. It is essential, in a public speaking situation, that your body language should reflect a confident personality with a good sense of humour. In order to achieve this you should think about the following:

Use of hands

■ Use your hands to emphasize what you say and to invite the audience to accept your point

■ Keep your hands open and keep your fingers open.

■ Avoid putting your hands in your pocket and avoid closing them. Firmly avoid pointing fingers

■ Co-ordinate your hand movements with your words.

Using facial expressions

People tend to concentrate on the face of a public speaker, in addition to the movements of the body. Obviously, your face, along with body language is a vehicle for expression. A smile every now and again is important. There are other actions that can help:

■ Use of eyebrows for inviting people to accept your ideas

■ Moving the head to look at all members of a group. very important indeed to maintain a sense of involvement on the part of all

■ Do not fix your eyes on one place or person for long. This will isolate the rest of the audience and may be interpreted as nervousness or a lack of confidence on your part

■ Look at individuals every time you mention something in their area of expertise or are singling them out in a positive way

■ Look at people even if they appear not to be looking at you

The face is a very important part of the communication apparatus and the use of this part of the body is of the utmost importance when public speaking.

Controlling your movements
In addition to the use of face and hands the way you move can have an effect on your audience. Your movements can vary from standing rigid and fixed to acting out roles and being fluid

generally. There are, in keeping with body language generally, certain rules relating to movement:

- Restrict your movements only to those that are most necessary. Avoid throwing yourself all over the place and distracting peoples attention from the emphasis of your presentation

- Always face the people that you are addressing. Never look at the floor or away from the audience, at least not for a prolonged period of time

Dress

When adopting the role of public speaker it is very important to be dressed formally and in accordance with the standard of the occasion, or the nature of the occasion. Dressing formally does not mean automatically wearing a suit and tie. It does mean however that you should think in terms of power dressing. This means that you wish to make an impression on people, not just through what you say and do, not just through body language or visual presentation but by the way you look. People must be impressed. This means that you must give thought to what you wear, how you can help to achieve a sense of control through dress.

Attitude

Your attitude is crucial to your success in public speaking. Attitudes can be greatly influenced by nerves and by being ill prepared. There is nothing worse than a public speaker who slowly degenerates into aggression or hostility through sarcasm or other forms of attack. Yet this is all too frequent. At all times you must maintain a professional and formal attitude that allows you to remain in control. You can think yourself into this state if you find yourself slipping or feel that you are losing control.

If you feel that you are straying in any way then you should get back on course. This can be achieved through a number of ways such as by changing the subject slightly in order to give yourself time to gather your wits or by asking the group to refocus on the subject in question.

Attitude is also disciplined by self-composure that can be engendered through relaxation that in turn is brought about by understanding the role of exercise and meditation, which we will be elaborating on a little later.

Formalities

Another fundamental rule of presentation is the way you open or introduce the presentation and the way you close. When public speaking it is always necessary to introduce yourself even if most of the audience know who you are. It is vital that everyone knows who you are, who you represent, if anybody, and what you are there for. Having got these necessary formalities over with, the audience will feel more comfortable listening to you because they now have a point of reference. Depending on the situation, you may even want to ask the audience if they would like to introduce themselves, through a "round robin" which entails each person telling you and the others who they are and what they hope to get out of the presentation. This approach however, is only really necessary and useful in seminar or teaching situations. Such an approach would be wholly inappropriate in a speech situation.

Practicing presentations

Taking into account all of the above and then practicing. This is the absolute key to successful presentations and to effective public speaking. Practice most certainly lifts your confidence level up and assists you in staying in control.

The more time and effort that you spend practicing the less that you will have to worry about when presenting. Lets face it, a presentation is a live stage show. How do stand up comics feel when they expose themselves to an audience? Develop a practicing technique by trying different methods:

- You should choose a topic that you are very interested in and prepare a short presentation on it.

- Stand in front of a mirror and present to yourself. Repeat this over and over, observing aspects of your style.

- Try to rectify any bad habits.

- Experiment with various styles and techniques until you find one that suits you.

- Try to film yourself if possible. Replay the film and observe yourself. This is one of the most effective ways of changing your style, or developing your style.

- Ask a friend to observe you and to make detailed criticism. Do not be afraid of criticism as this always constructive

At this point you should be concentrating on style only. Do not worry about content as we will be discussing this a little later.

Now read the key points from chapter four.

**

KEY POINTS FROM CHAPTER FOUR

- Body language emphasises speech and helps us to communicate more effectively with others
- Visual stimuli is equally as important when public speaking
- It is very important to develop your own style as a public speaker
- The use of language is a specific medium which must be understood when public speaking
- Formal but simple language interspersed with funny remarks is one of the best ways to approach an audience
- The use of facial expressions is very important when addressing others
- The way you move can have a very important effect on an audience
- Adopt an appropriate mode of dress for the audience you are addressing. It is better to be smart than scruffy
- Your attitude is crucial to your success as a public speaker
- The way you open and close your presentation is of the utmost importance
- You should always practice presentations before the event

CHAPTER 5

THE USE OF VISUAL AIDS

Before we further discuss presentation of your material it is necessary to talk a little about the use of visual aids. Although many speeches are carried out without the use of visuals, it is surprising what a difference they can make.

When making a speech, visual aids are used for effect, for helping you to make your point. They offer audiences a visual representation of what you are trying to put across. Generally, you can explain a point much quicker with the use of such aids.

Visual aids also keep audiences interested, as there is more entertainment value with the use of visual images than there is with the spoken word. Combined with words, visual aids help you to communicate ideas in a very short time and leave a longer lasting impression on the audience. This is only true though if you use them to their best effect. The opposite can have a detrimental effect on the audience.

Visual aids are not effective if they are not prepared very carefully together with the script that you are presenting. Do not try to overload the visual aid in terms of its contents or this will, more often than not, confuse your audience. Whether you use a graph, diagram or picture on the slide (if it is a slide that you are using) then put only one on each slide. When working on the main body of the slide keep the following in mind:

- Keep it as simple as possible

- Use pictures as often as you can keeping text to a minimum

- Leave plenty of space between items for visibility

- Use professional images (computer generated) as opposed to hand drawn

Throughout your presentation, try to use the same style for visual aids.

Presenting with visual images
Images are there to help you and you should be comfortable with using the equipment that displays them.

The following tips are useful when presenting:

■ Ignore the existence of a picture behind you. Never turn your back on the audience. Talk to them at the same time as they are looking at the image.

■ Always rehearse with your visual aids. This will help you to familiarize yourself with the equipment and also to remember the sequence in which you will present the slides

■ If you are going to use an overhead projector, make sure that all your acetates are in order. Put them back in the same order when you finish so that they are ready for use next time. Keep them clean.

■ Stand to one side of the overhead projector when you are presenting. Use a pointer to make a relevant point.

■ Let the audience see where you are pointing your pointer

Tools for the presentation of visual aids

Use of an Overhead projector and use of power point

This particular tool is the most popular of all visual aids. It is widely used in all forms of presentations because of its flexibility. It can be used to project almost any form of material. However, more and more people use power point as a presentation tool as it is slick and more professional.

Slide projectors

This is the second most popular tool for visual aids. The quality is always very good, often much better than the OHP. However, it can be more expensive to produce materials than the OHP.

Using a video

This is the most effective visual aid but should be used only for limited periods. More information can be shown in a short space of time than other forms of visual aids.

Use of other visual aids

In addition to the main method chosen by yourself there are other peripheral visual aids which you may wish to utilise. The following are also quite effective:

- *Flip chart.* This particular tool enables you to write and draw as you go along.

■ *Models and prototypes.* Showing a model is very powerful when trying to demonstrate a particular point. Displaying models of buildings can be more effective than showing plans.

Use of colour

Colour is also a very powerful medium when you wish to make important information stand out. The audience can focus on the coloured parts with the background information remaining in the background.

Working with computers

Computers play an important part in presentations. Whether you are making or presenting slides, the results look more professional and effective with the use of presentation or graphics software.

Choosing the right equipment

It is important to use the right kind of visual aids for each occasion. If used incorrectly, visual aids can give the wrong impression or even ruin your chances of success in getting your message across.

Choosing the right visual aid is quite difficult.

The following (overleaf) are points to consider:

- The ability to grab the audience's attention. There is no point using the most impressive equipment if it will not appeal to the audience

- The suitability for the occasion. You do not need to use state of the art equipment if you are giving a short speech. Use the most appropriate form of equipment

- The effect of your visual aids on the audience. Will the visual aid that you intend to use help or just confuse the audience. You should very carefully ensure that what you use perfectly compliments your presentation.

Use of notes and handouts

It is sometimes useful to provide your audience with a handout of your presentation, or part of your presentation. This very much depends on what you are presenting or whether you are making a simple speech. Only provide handouts when needed and not at the start of the presentation as this will distract the audience from what it is you are trying to say and also the content of any visual aid.

Involving the audience

Sometimes you may wish to involve the audience in an interactive presentation. If you need to make a quick survey or opinion poll to prove a point, you can pass a short questionnaire to the audience and let someone help you in counting the votes and presenting.

Always remember, visual aids are there to assist you in presenting your message and if they don't achieve that don't bother with them.

Now read the key points from chapter five

**

KEY POINTS FROM CHAPTER FIVE

- Visual aids are for effect, for helping you to make your point

- Visual aids are not effective if they are not prepared in line with the material that you are presenting

- Keep visual aids as simple as possible

- Use professional images

- When presenting, stand to one side to enable the audience to see what it is you are presenting

- Select carefully the tool for presenting the visual aids

- The use of notes and handouts can be important in some cases

---

CHAPTER 6

EFFECTIVE DELIVERY- THE VOICE

We need to consider one of the most important aspects of public speaking before we move on to actual presentation.

What you say is very important indeed. However, even more important is the way that you say it. The right combination of body language and voice is far more potent than a clever and witty script. The two combined can help you become a very effective public speaker indeed.

The voice

The voice plays a very important role in presentation and public speaking generally. The way you pitch your voice is guaranteed to either keep peoples attention or send them to sleep.

The voice is a result of air coming out of your lungs which causes the vocal chords to vibrate, producing different sounds. These various sounds are shaped into words by the speech organism in the head.

The brain then sends messages controlling the breathing and tension of the vocal chords. Cavities in the body, such as the mouth and chest, provide amplification. The amplified sounds are then shaped into recognizable speech by the tongue, lips teeth etc. Speech is produced in two different ways:

- Voiced sounds-produced by speech organs in the mouth closer to the vocal chords at the back end of the tongue

- Unvoiced sounds-produced mainly using the tongue and front teeth. The sound of the letter S is produced in this way.

All the above aspects of voice and speech are controlled by the body organs that are unique to each person. We can develop the ability to control these organs to produce the speech that we want. This can be achieved by training the various muscles that produce and shape sounds. The shape of various cavities, such as the chest, can be changed to vary the level of sound amplification.

Developing your voice

It is perfectly possible, and probably essential to improve on four characteristics of your speech:

- tone
- pitch
- volume
- clarity.

Tone

If you restrict your body cavities responsible for amplifying sound, your voice will sound restricted sometimes nasal. Restriction of body cavities can happen by standing or sitting in the wrong way.

It is essential that you give thought to your posture and bearing when in public speaking

Pitch

As you stretch and loosen your voice chords, the pitch of your voice will change. When stretched. the number of vibrations increases due to the small distance allowed for them to vibrate. These vibrations produce high frequency (pitch) sounds.

When the vocal chords are loose, more distance is allowed for them to vibrate which makes them produce low frequency (pitch) sound.

Volume

The volume of your voice can be improved in two ways. The first is by simply increasing the pressure of air coming out of your lungs, or by narrowing the space between the vocal chords (glottis). You can change the volume of a whisper simply by increasing the amount of air through your glottis which is widely open. Try to shout. You will notice that your glottis contracts sharply, to increase the volume of your voice.

Clarity

To get your message across you need to say it clearly. Clarity is determined by speech organs and how well you can control them. If you are too nervous your tongue and lips start playing tricks on you because they are tense. In order to speak clearly, overcome the problems associated with speech organs and get your message across. Don't be scared of moving your lips. Exercise your speech muscles. Make sure that you pronounce things clearly and that you carry your voice.

Voice pitch

People generally feel more comfortable listening to a deep voice, one that is well rounded and smooth. However, it is important to ensure that your voice is at your natural pitch and not forced. To find your natural pitch, concentrate on the following exercises:

- Speak at the lowest note that feels comfortable to you

- Use a musical instrument, e.g. a guitar or piano and find the note that corresponds to your lowest comfortable pitch

- Move four notes up the musical scale. This should be very close to your natural pitch

- Try to tune your voice with this note and speak with the music helping you to stay in tune

- Practice this as many times as you need, in order to become confident in finding your pitch quite quickly.

When you have found the natural pitch of your voice, you will need to work on some variations to make your speech more natural. Changing the pitch up and down according to the contents of the speech helps you to keep the audience attracted to what you are saying. Try saying a few sentences out loud and practice varying the pitch. You can then notice the relation between the contents of the sentences and your pitch when saying each of them. When you realize what you are capable of achieving with your voice, you can then consciously start varying the pitch. Singing is very good for voice training and realizing the potential of your voice organs. Reading out loud and trying to act a story is also good training.

Use of silences and pauses:

Sometimes, silence can be more effective than words. It is useful to pause every now and again to allow the listeners to absorb the ideas that you have put across. A short pause gives the audience time to absorb what you have said. You can also use pauses to help you relax and breath. Pauses also help you put your ideas together to start elaborating on a new point.

A few useful hints on the use of pauses:

■ Don't feel compelled to fill the silence. If you find yourself speaking quickly for no real reason, force yourself to pause. Sometimes you may be very enthusiastic about what you are saying and find yourself speaking rapidly. Pause and use your body language and voice to show your enthusiasm

■ Avoid becoming a slow speaker. Moderate the speed of your talk to the level of its contents. Always remember that the aim is to be understood and not to say as many words as possible within the given time.

■ Try to maintain the rhythm and the rate of flow of ideas throughout your presentation. Again this can be achieved by practicing your presentation enough times to make you feel confident and in command.

Emphasis

There are other ways to emphasize a point or an idea. The amount of stress put on a syllable can also emphasize a word. You should say certain sentences, placing emphasis on different words.

A few examples are:

- Can I have that *chair* please
- Can I have *that* chair please

In the first sentence you are asked for the chair and not something else. In the second sentence, you want the specific chair to be given to you and not someone else. Therefore, placing the stress on a word can change the whole sentence. Avoid putting emphasis on too many words. This diminishes the effect of the technique and renders it useless.

It is important to realize that emphasis in many cases is placed on a group of words rather than just one. The same technique applies, but in the case of a group of words, the pitch change to the decisive tone can be extended to include all the words in the group. The whole group should be treated as one entity with the emphasis on the group and not the individual words.

Voice projection

Voice projection depends on two main factors:

- Physical
- Psychological

The physical factor comprises

- The force with which you breath
- The muscular power you put into forming the words
- The clarity of your pronunciation

If you get all these factors right then you will have no problem projecting your voice. However, some people feel nervous in front of audience and they fail to project their voice properly. In a lot of cases speakers project their voices too much or too little simply because they do not look at the audience and estimate the power that they need to project. In order to estimate projection, you should look at the person the furthest away from you and imagine that you are talking too him or her. You will feel the need to project your voice to that person and be able to control your vocal organs and breathing accordingly.

Use of the body

To help you to project your voice, you should make use of the resonance of your body cavities.

Try the following:

1. Relax the muscles in your neck and stand comfortably without bending or over straightening your chest.

2. Also relax the muscles in your neck by nodding gently a few times.

3. Take a deep breath and exhale, letting out a deep sound. You can then realize how the cavity in your chest resonates giving out a sigh of relief

The nose

A clear nose helps you to speak clearly and project your voice. If your nose is blocked, it is harder for you to pronounce certain letters let alone project your voice. It is also easier to breath through a clear nose and therefore maintain the breathing rhythm.

Improving posture

Other cavities in the body, such as the chest, can be used to create more resonance. It helps if your posture is right. For a good posture try the following:

- Relax your muscles especially around the shoulder area. To do so you need to raise your shoulders and drop them a few times.

- Do not bend forward as you speak. This prevents your chest cavity from resonating

- If you stand with a curved back and too stiff you will not be able to project your voice properly

- Relax your body and stand in a natural position. This will help you not only project your voice but maintain it for a longer time too.

Training and looking after your voice

Changing your speech habits that have developed over a number of years is not a simple matter. You need to consciously work at this before the changes become second nature to you.

You should always look after your voice in order to maintain it:

- Avoid smoky rooms

- Allow your voice to rest. Even when you are giving a long talk or speech, you can still rest your voice by regular breathing and proper articulation

- Avoid warm and dry rooms which can bring on a sore throat

- Don't eat dairy products before your presentation, because the production of mucus is increased which roughens the voice

■ If you feel that you have a dry mouth and throat, bite your tongue gently. This will produce enough saliva to wet your mouth

■ After a long talk, practice a few relaxing exercises to prepare your voice for rest. These exercises can be stretching, breathing articulation etc.

Now read the key points from chapter Six overleaf

**

KEY POINTS FROM CHAPTER SIX

- The voice plays an all important part in presentations

- It is essential to improve characteristics of speech-tone, volume and clarity

- The use of silence and pauses is very effective when public speaking

- Voice projection is vital when speaking

- If your posture is right this enhances the ability to project your voice

---

CHAPTER 7

EXERCISES GENERALLY

Exercises to help you relax

Although at first glance exercising may seem to have very little to do with public speaking, in fact the reverse is true. There are certain exercises which are essential to your posture and general well-being. If you are aware of these simple routines and can go through the motions just prior to embarking on public speaking, then you will feel so much better.

Shoulders

In order to feel relaxed, you should stand in a relaxed position, lift the shoulders and tense them. Slowly relax them by letting them fall. You should then note the difference in the way you feel. Sometimes we lift our shoulders and tense them without realizing that we are doing so. When your shoulders are tense, the neck becomes tense and you can feel very uncomfortable and tire more easily.

Neck

Neck exercises are very beneficial in the process of relaxation. Move your head gently round from left to right in a circular motion. Imagine that you are repeating this exercise in front of an audience. This is particularly useful for releasing tension and should be carried out just prior to beginning your presentation.

Head

In a standing position, let the head very slowly fall onto your chest. Repeat this for a few times and you feel very light and relaxed. The contrast between lightness and the heaviness which is experienced when your head is kept in a normal position over prolonged periods of time can be felt very easily.

Concentration

This particular exercise is useful for focusing the mind. Choose an interesting object that appeals to you. Fix your mind on it taking in as much detail as possible. Rest your head against the back of the chair close your eyes and place the image of that object in your mind. When you are ready, open your eyes. Carrying out this particular exercise is useful prior to public speaking.

Breathing control

Breathing, for any form of presentation, is a natural function that we do not normally think about. If you find it difficult to project your voice in public, concentrating on breathing will work wonders for you. To be heard by an audience, we need to create space in the throat and chest so that the required amount of air can be freely inhaled. When using the voice, the exhaled air is directed through the vocal cords. The throat, mouth and nose help us to amplify our sound. The mouth and throat should therefore be free of tension, and the nose kept clear and unblocked for the resonators to operate effectively.

Breathing in

For this exercise, you should stand straight but not stiffly. Good posture helps promote strong voice production. Remember when you inhale not to raise the shoulders. Doing so will encourage tension in the neck, throat and breathing muscles.

Now you should feel your ribcage. Ribs form the thorax and are attached at the back to the twelve thoracic vertebrae. Rest one hand on your midriff and the other on your lower ribs that reach around the waist. Breathe in slowly and notice how the hand resting on the midriff moves out slightly. This has happened because the diaphragm, which is a muscular partition that separates the thorax from the abdomen, has contracted and flattened, thereby pushing the belly outwards. Because the lower ribs are more flexible than those higher up, they will flex outwards and upwards by the use of intercostal muscles that are attached to them.

This muscular activity expands the chest cavity, creating more space for the lungs to fill up with air, which is drawn into them through the windpipe, nose and/or mouth.

Breathing out

You should now breath out very slowly and feel the lower ribs gradually relax as the lungs contract. The diaphragm rises and the midriff or belly moves inwards. As this is happening, the abdominal muscles are gently drawn inwards. This contraction of the abdominal muscles is used to help our outgoing breath when we speak, gently supporting the diaphragm and lower ribs, so that sound can be sustained and energized.

Because it is on the outgoing breath that we speak, we aim to balance breath with sound. The moment we start to exhale, we need to use the voice. This can be achieved by humming. This will help you to attain smoothness.

Physical tensions and feelings of nervousness can be increased or even caused by insufficient intake of air. At times, this can result in a sore throat, breathy or strained voice and tailing off at the ends of sentences. Some speakers do not allow themselves breathing space. They take in small gasps of air and do not take advantage of their breathing muscles. The shoulders may rise on inhalation, which encourages the ribs to move one-way only (vertically) and this can constrict the breath. The ribs need to flex vertically and laterally. Raising the arms slightly to the side while practicing breathing in may provide a picture of opening out, so that lateral expansion is encouraged.

The voice generally

As we have discussed, when speaking in public, the voice needs to be strong and powerful without straining or shouting. You need to get the message home to people in a clear confident way. Your breath is the power behind your voice. It is important to inhale as much as possible. The aim is to flow and we breath when there are pauses in the text.

In order to make sense of content, learn where to punctuate your speech and phrase your words. Do not break your phrases or your speech will become jerky and the sense may be lost.

When your speech is prepared, practice it aloud and initially gauge where you are going to take:

■ Your full stop pauses

■ Your comma pauses and supplementary breaths

Ensure that you are standing straight but be at ease, especially around the top part of your body, the neck, throat and shoulders, which should be relaxed and down. Stand with legs

75

slightly apart, the weight evenly distributed on both feet. Your head needs to be well balanced between the shoulder blades. The chin should not jut out or be pushed too far into the neck. If you were speaking to a fairly large audience you would need to speak a little slower and very clearly.

The above represents a few key exercises that you should become familiar with if you wish to increase your effectiveness as a public speaker and become aware of your posture and your physical self generally.

Now read the key points from chapter 7 overleaf.

**

KEY POINTS FROM CHAPTER 7

■ Although at first glance exercising may seem to have very little to do with public speaking, in fact the reverse is true. There are certain exercises that are essential to your posture and general well being.

■ Shoulder, neck and head exercises are very important in the process of relaxation.

■ Breathing, for any form of presentation, is a natural function that we do not normally think about. If you find it difficult to project your voice in public, concentrating on breathing will work wonders for you.

■ As we have discussed in chapter 6, when speaking in public, the voice needs to be strong and powerful without straining or shouting. You need to get the message home to people in a clear confident way. Your breath is the power behind your voice.

CHAPTER 8

A FEW HINTS ON SETTING

By now, you should have gained a reasonably clear idea of the ground work that you must do before you are ready to stand in front of others and deliver an effective speech or make an effective presentation. In addition, you will have gained some idea of the importance of physical exercise and its relation to your own well being. However, before you begin your presentation it will do no harm in considering the type of environment that you will present in.

Choosing the right setting

There are a number of types of places where you may find yourself giving a presentation. These can vary from a small, over ventilated room to a large and comfortable seminar room.

For a good setting a room should posses the following:

- It should be large enough to accommodate all present]

- The temperature should be just right and not uncomfortable (too hot or too warm or too cold)

■ All seats should be positioned correctly

■ Enough space should be provided for visual aids]

■ Lighting should be controllable

■ There should be enough power points close to the location of your equipment

■ The acoustics should be suitable.

If you have the chance to go into a room some time before the presentation, look out for aspects which can be improved upon and which bring the room in line with the above criteria.

Further tips are:

■ Close any windows that overlook a busy street, to avoid noise pollution in the room. If the room is too warm and you need to open a window, do so before the presentation and close them just before you start.

■ If the room is small, with an elevated platform for the presenter to stand on, arrange the seating to give you enough space in front of the platform. Use this space and avoid standing at a higher level than your small audience. This can only intimidate them and create barriers.

■ If you can rearrange the seating in the room, always try to place the seats facing you with their back to the room door. This enables latecomers to sneak in without distracting people's attention from you

■ In large lecture theatres, make sure that the lighting is controlled, so that when you start your presentation, it is dimmed in the audience section. This helps the audience focus on you and your visual aids.

■ However, it should not be too dark for the audience to take notes if necessary.

**

CHAPTER 9

DEALING WITH NERVES

We briefly discussed public speaking and nervousness at the beginning of this book. However, now that the big day has approached, you may be feeling more nervous than ever. Therefore, it is necessary to look at nerves in more detail.

Fear need not become an obstacle to your success as a speaker. In fact, nervousness can become a positive aid to your ability to put across your message, as long as you learn to take control of it.

Perseverance in the face of fear

In moments of panic it might be difficult to remember why it ever occurred to you to speak in public. Thousands of people stand up in front of audiences every day. Each of these individuals has a different reason for doing it-teachers, sales people, lawyers and so on-the list is endless. When they go out and address their audience they are fulfilling their own and their audiences needs.

Learning the skills to be a successful public speaker has many advantages:

- You become more effective in your workplace

- You are better able to recall important facts and figures.

- You are better equipped to research information

- You become more widely knowledgeable as a result of keeping a close eye on the media

- You are better able to argue your point.

- You are better able to communicate with people on many different levels

- You can improve your interview or selling technique

■ You may find that other people consider you more interesting and seek out your company more often

■ You may be able to persuade people to a good cause

■ You may find yourself making people laugh-one of the greatest gifts of all

Whatever your reason, remember it when you are beset by nerves. If you have a good enough reason to speak in public, you will succeed in fulfilling your audiences needs and your own.

Fear of public speaking

The best way to describe how a person feels when they are frightened is to list a number of symptoms: sweating, blushing, racing pulse, clumsiness or shaking limbs and a blank mind. The key to fighting debilitating fear is to think beyond the symptoms to the cause. When asked to list reasons why they may feel fear when faced with speaking in public, the following are often listed as reasons:

■ I am inexperienced

■ I do not know enough about the subject

■ I am afraid of the audience

- My mind may go blank

- The equipment may go wrong

- I may make a complete fool of myself by saying or doing something stupid

- All of these worries are founded on one fear: the fear of the unknown

As a novice speaker, making your debut, you may consider yourself in a particularly frightening situation. However, every speaker you have ever heard once made a maiden speech. The fear of the novice quickly disintegrates as soon as that maiden speech is over, so you might as well take the bull by the horns and do it now.

What else is there in the speaking situation that is unknown, and therefore to be feared? You may feel that you do not know your subject well enough, or that you may lose your thread half way through or that your mind will go blank. It is in your power to get rid of this fear by thorough preparation.

If you are not sure of your subject, take action to change it. You may be able to do this by narrowing the field by covering only those subjects of which you are certain. If you think that you might lose your way, take time to rehearse well in advance, so that you can extemporize with ease. Extemporization is merely elaborating a theme. If you know your subject well enough, if you have planned your speech logically, and if you have made good memory jogging notes, you should have no fear of not finding your way back to the right path should you stray for a moment.

Equally, there is no excuse for the fear that your equipment might fail you. Familiarity with the equipment you intend to use and thorough checking of what is available at the venue should put your mind at rest. If you feel terror at the thought of your audience, usually the biggest fear, you should remember that your audience is looking forward to hearing you, they would like to hear you speak and they are expecting you to fulfil at least one of their needs. If you are truly sure of your subject matter then you can speak to any audience with confidence.

Remember, you are the one in charge, you are the one who has control and will deliver a speech that others will enjoy and remember. This is the attitude that you should have, not over confident but just right-at ease and relaxed, comfortable with yourself, and in command of your subject matter.

Relate the art of public speaking to that of an everyday conversation. Very rarely do you lose control of an everyday conversation. There is no reason why you should think any differently of public speaking.

Practical ways of controlling fear

Fear is merely the product of lack of preparation. However, fear is not a rational sentiment, it is a physical response and, try as you might, you cannot banish it. An alternative way of tackling anxiety is through the body, rather than through the brain. People are more prone to anxiety in certain circumstances, and if you can avoid those circumstances then it is possible to reduce stress significantly.

General health

Because fear is a physical reaction, people often find that, when they are feeling below par, they become anxious about trivial things. In the days before your speech, rest and eat properly and keep off alcohol. Take a couple of brisk walks.

Try to avoid stimulants such as caffeine, cigarettes, etc. Try to relax naturally and learn a good breathing exercise.

In seeking to reduce your anxiety, it is not necessary to eradicate it altogether. A taste of nerves keeps your mind alert. It is important to keep on your toes if you are to appear at your best.

Most of all, remember that you have very little to lose and a lot to gain by speaking in public.

Now read the key points from Chapter 9 overleaf.

Now read the key points from Chapter 9 overleaf.

**

KEY POINTS FROM CHAPTER 9

■ Fear need not become an obstacle to your success as a speaker. In fact, nervousness can become a positive aid to your ability to put across your message, as long as you learn to take control of it.

■ The best way to describe how a person feels when they are frightened is to list a number of symptoms: sweating, blushing, racing pulse, clumsiness or shaking limbs and a blank mind. The key to fighting debilitating fear is to think beyond the symptoms to the cause.

■ Fear is merely the product of lack of preparation. However, fear is not a rational sentiment, it is a physical response and, try as you might, you cannot banish it. Therefore, make sure that you are adequately prepared.

■ As a novice speaker, making your debut, you may consider yourself in a particularly frightening situation. However, every speaker you have ever heard once made a maiden speech. The fear of the novice quickly disintegrates as soon as that maiden speech is over.

CHAPTER 10

DELIVERING YOUR PRESENTATION

All that you have read has been leading to one main point: that is the day of your speech. The following should be noted in order to avoid things going wrong:

In the week before the event you should contact the organizers in order to ensure that the event is still taking place and that nothing has changed.

You should ensure the following:

- You have the name and address of the venue. A simple matter but crucial

- Travel arrangements. Things such as parking and those who will meet you

- Contact name and telephone number in case you are held up on the day

- Time of the event

■ Dress requirements

■ Length of speech

■ Names of anyone to be mentioned, for example, in a toast

■ Any special facilities required by yourself should be checked beforehand

The eve of your speech

The eve of your speech is the time to check the contents of your speech, once again, and carry out any possible rehearsals. Make sure that you have checked any equipment that you are going to take with you and any visual aids. Make sure that you know what clothes you are going to wear and then try to relax.

The key to the whole night before is ensuring that you have all you need, it is in working order and you are fully prepared. Then it is time to meditate. Try not to dwell on what you have to do the next day. Your subconscious is doing that for you anyway.

The day

It is essential that you give yourself enough time to reach your destination. Always leave yourself an extra half an hour so that you arrive well in advance. You will need this time to make any arrangements that are necessary prior to carrying out the speech.

You will also have to meet relevant people. Before you leave for the venue make sure that you have everything with you. Check that you have things like cue cards that you may be using as a prompt. Be very careful at this point. Stop and think before you leap!

Arrival

As soon as you arrive you should make contact with the organizers and run through the running order of the day with them, establishing the start and finish times and also whether there have been any changes.

At the earliest opportunity, pay a visit to the room that you will be speaking in. As we have seen, the venue is all important.

Socializing

After you have checked the venue, you may be asked to socialize. This can be a very useful time. If members of the audience see that you are mingling with them in an affable sort of way, you will reinforce the feeling that you are friendly and sympathetic and that you are interested in the people and the event. It will also take your mind off your speech and help you to judge the mood of your audience.

If you are offered a drink you should ensure that you do not get tipsy. Eat sparingly.

If you are in the room when people are taking their seats you should keep an eye on the distribution. A small audience that is scattered across a large auditorium is going to be more difficult to handle than people who are in a tight group.

A few minutes before you are due to speak begin to prepare yourself. Make sure that you feel fresh. Take a trip to the lavatory if necessary. If you have to sit through other people's speeches, be alert and interested. You will probably be just as visible as the person speaking and you should do nothing to distract the audience's attention. You may also need to edit your speech.

When it is time to go on, and you are being introduced, look at the introducer and be alert. While the introduction is being made, breathe deeply and concentrate on the opening words of your speech. When the introduction is over, get into position, make yourself comfortable and check that you have the audience's attention, smile and begin. If you are using the same space as a previous speaker then make sure that any remnants of their speech is removed, such as chalk on blackboard etc.

Dealing with hecklers

Some people come to meetings with the sole aim of disrupting the person speaking. Others may become rowdy after drink. Dealing with such people is a key skill and totally essential if you wish to convey your message.

You should observe the audience beforehand in order to spot such people. Ignore initial heckling attempt a witty put-down if repeated. Keep your sense of humour at all times. Demonstrate maturity and professionalism. Only if a heckler becomes extremely abusive should you think about having him or her ejected.

Question time

You may find yourself in a situation, depending on the occasion, where the audience can put questions to you. The best time for questions is when you have finished your speech so that you are not disrupted. When you take a question, listen carefully and try to repeat it. This is not only so that the audience can hear it but also so that you can frame your answer.

Spend as much time as you can with questioners who are being constructive, conversely, make sure that those who are repetitive or who ramble are stopped in their tracks.

Finally

Ensure that you stay in control at all times. Ensure that all the preliminaries have been taken care of, you are dressed correctly, you are confident, know your subject, have researched it and pieced it together well and that you grab the audience's attention. Ensure that your speech is totally relevant to the occasion. After you have delivered your speech, regardless of whether it has been successful or not, you will have a sense of well-being.

Good luck with your maiden speech!

Now read the key points from chapter ten overleaf.

KEY POINTS FROM CHAPTER TEN

- Contact the organizers one week before the event in order to ensure that all is running smoothly and that you are still speaking

- On the eve of your speech, carry out rehearsals in order to get yourself in the right state of mind

- Give yourself plenty of time to reach your destination

- If you socialize prior to your speech, ensure that you do not drink too much

- When you embark upon your speech, ensure that you know how to handle the audience, in particular how to handle hecklers

- Ensure that you allow time for questions after

- Above all, relax!

Chapter 11

REMOTE PRESENTATIONS-ZOOM

Now that more people are working from home, online presentations using tools like Zoom have started to become the norm. However, giving a Zoom presentation is very different from presenting in person. The lack of physical presence and body language can make it difficult to engage and inspire your audience.

Preparing Your Zoom Presentation

Getting ready for your Zoom presentation is just as important as giving the actual presentation. There are lots of potential issues you can face, like a faulty microphone or your dog walking in right in the middle of an important slide.

By preparing well, you ensure your presentation is as smooth and error-free as possible. After all, you only get one chance to make a great first. Below are some tips to help you get ready to deliver a powerful and effective Zoom presentation.

1. Design an Effective Online Presentation

The first thing you need to do is make sure your presentation is designed to look its best on your audiences' tiny computer screens. Follow the three rules below to create an effective Zoom presentation.

Keep it simple.

The best online presentations are simple and straightforward. You don't want your audience to be squinting at their screens trying to navigate through a tangled web of text, colors, graphs and other content. You need them to look at a slide and get the point at a single glance.

Use a plain background for your slides, preferably white, and focus each slide on only one point or idea. Don't stuff too many bullet points or text into your slides.

Also, make sure you center your text in case the edges of the slides are cut off for some of the participants.

Lastly, use a large and bold font that doesn't require participants to strain their eyes, even if they're viewing your slides on their phone.

Use relevant visuals.

Visuals make information much easier to digest and retain than plain text. And let's face it—they keep things entertaining. Below are some types of visuals you can use to make your Zoom presentation more engaging:

Charts and graphs. Visualizing data can bring the most boring numbers and statistics to life. If you're using research findings to show a trend or back up your point, consider presenting them in the form of a bar graph or pie chart. Not only will it add some color to your slides, it will make it easier for your audience to interpret the data.

Maps. If you're presenting geographic data, you can easily visualize it in the form of maps.

Icons and illustrations. Adding creative graphics like icons and illustrations can break up walls of text, make your information look more visual and interesting, and help explain your point better.

Videos. Adding videos into your slides is a great way to make your presentation more engaging. Videos can help you explain a point more clearly, show a product in action or give some background information on your subject. You can embed YouTube videos into your slides or upload them directly.

Stock photos. If used intelligently, stock photos can add value to your slides by helping you set the tone, tell a story or visualize an idea. You can also use relevant stock photos in the background with text overlay to add some color to your slides.

GIFs and Memes. Make your online presentations fun and engaging by adding relevant memes and GIFs into slides that would otherwise look quite dry. Be careful not to overdo it, and only use humor if appropriate. You don't want to risk looking unprofessional.

Using visuals in your online presentation is great, but this doesn't mean you should stuff all your slides with images. Make sure the visuals you're using add value to your content and emphasize your point instead of taking attention away from it.

Make it interactive.

It can be tough to keep your audience engaged when you're not interacting with them face-to-face. So, why not do the next best thing? Make your slides interactive. Below are a few tips.

Animation. Add beautiful slide transitions, or animate objects separately. A good tip is to animate bullet points to appear one at a time to draw focus to each one. You can also choose from pre-animated illustrations, icons and characters to make your Zoom presentation more engaging.

Links. You can link any text or graphic element to a web page, or a slide or object inside your presentation. Get creative with this tool to add interactive quizzes, slides and more to your Zoom presentation. For example, you can link two text boxes together so when you click on the question, the answer appears.

Hover effects. If you're linking one object in your slide to another, you can enable it to show up on either click or hover. If you're creating a quiz, for example, you can link two text boxes together so when you hover on the question, the answer appears.

A healthy dose of interactivity can make your audience feel more involved with your Zoom presentation.

2 Tidy Up Your Background

If you want your audience to take you seriously, clean up any clutter behind you. A messy background can make you look unprofessional and distract people from focusing on your presentation. Ideally, your background should be a plain wall.

If you can't manage to find a clean, empty background, consider using a virtual Zoom background. There are lots of different styles out there, so make sure to pick one that looks realistic and professional.

3 Draw Attention to Your Face

An online presentation can quickly start to feel distant and impersonal, like watching a pre-recorded video. To remind your audience that they're interacting with a real human, you need to draw focus to your face and expressions as you present. Make sure you're presenting in a well-lit room, where the source of light is in front of you. If the light source is directly behind you, you might end up looking like a dark blob.

4 Check Your Equipment

Make sure you check all your technical equipment to see if everything is working properly. This will help minimize issues like awkward camera angles or a malfunctioning microphone.

Here are a few things you should take care of before your presentation:

Check your internet connection. No one wants to listen to a presenter with laggy audio and video. Use a reliable, high-speed internet connection to ensure a smooth Zoom presentation.

Test audio and video. Check if your camera and microphone are working properly by joining a Zoom test meeting. You can also test out your equipment from inside the Zoom app by clicking on *Settings → Audio* or *Settings → Video*.

Ensure your laptop is plugged in. Imagine if your laptop dies out in the middle of your presentation just because you didn't plug it in properly. Don't let that happen.

Adjust your camera level. Make sure your audience is looking at your face instead of the top of your head. Decide whether you want to sit or stand during your presentation, and adjust the webcam so it's at eye level.

Keep in mind that technical issues can arise unexpectedly, even if you do everything right. Doing tech prep beforehand, though, keeps the chances at a minimum.

5 Minimize Potential Interruptions

Whether you're giving your Zoom presentation at home or in a nearby cafe, there are lots of potential interruptions that can disrupt your flow and make you look unprofessional. During your preparations, your goal should be to minimize these interruptions as much as possible.

Find a quiet area to begin with, and lock the door so no one comes in unexpectedly. It's a good idea to inform your family members or others that you're going to be busy prior to the presentation.

Another tip is to close all other open applications and windows on your computer. Notifications and sounds can interrupt your meeting and distract you. You can also use the "Do Not Disturb" mode on MacOS or "Focus Assist" on Windows 10 to mute notifications.

6 Put Your Notes in the Right Place

Just like when you're presenting in person, you'd likely want to keep notes or pointers nearby in case you forget something important.

During a Zoom presentation, though, you need to be careful about where you place your notes. It can look very unprofessional and awkward if your eyes keep moving away from the camera when everyone is staring at your face.

Avoid keeping a notepad next to you or pasting them on the side of your monitor. A better alternative is to stick a post-it right below or next to your webcam. So, even if you take a peek, you will still be looking somewhat directly at your audience.

7. Delivering Your Zoom Presentation

Now that you're ready to give your Zoom presentation, here are some tips to help you make the most of your time while you're presenting.

Start With a Bang

It can take as little as five seconds to judge how charismatic a speaker is. Working out how to start your presentation is one of the most important parts of your Zoom presentation. It can either get your audience to sit up in their seats or prepare to doze off. Below are a few pointers:

Reveal a shocking statistic. A relevant and powerful statistic can set the tone for your presentation and show your audience the importance of your message.

Tell a relevant joke. Humor is a great way to break the ice and keep your audience engaged. A boring presentation can quickly cause the listener to zone out.

Ask a question. Get your audience involved by asking them a question relevant to your presentation topic. The more you interact with them, the more likely they'll be to listen to what you're saying.

Quote an influential person. A powerful quote can often motivate or inspire your audience to sit up and listen to what you have to say.

Tell a short story. Stories are personal and can evoke emotions. Telling a relatable story that also gets the audience curious to know more is a great way to start your presentation.

Use an interesting prop. Using a prop can break the monotony of your presentation. Using motion and a visual object can also help attract your audience's gaze.

Show a captivating visual. Pictures speak louder than words, which is why using a powerful image that tells a story or shows the importance of your topic is an effective way to start your presentation.

Along with starting impressively, you should also try to end your presentation in a way that it drives your audience to take action or think about your message. A good idea is to end with a powerful statement or a thought-provoking question.

8. Make Eye Contact With the Audience

While you're speaking, it's just as important to make eye contact with your audience as it is during a face-to-face presentation. The problem with Zoom presentations is that you often end up looking at your own video or at the video of your audience.

To make eye contact online you need to look directly at your camera. To make things easier, you can place the video boxes of your audience at the top of your screen, directly under your webcam.

9. Regularly Pause to Engage

Online presentations can get monotonous really quickly, and it's common for people to lose interest out in the middle of it. If you want to ensure your message hits home, take regular breaks throughout your Zoom presentation and engage your audience in conversation.

You could pause to ask them questions, or simply ask what they think about a certain topic. You could also try switching up the pace of your presentation, show a short video clip or tell an interesting or humorous story that helps bring wandering minds back.

10. Use the Chat Feature to Your Benefit

Zoom's chat feature is a great way to get your audience involved without disrupting the flow of your presentation. You can use Zoom chat to your advantage in several different ways:

Questions. Ask your audience questions and let them answer through chat, or get them to ask you questions in the chat.

Feedback. Let your audience know beforehand that they can leave their feedback and comments related to your presentation or topic in the chat. For example, if someone comments that they can't hear you properly you can try fixing your mic or raising your voice.

Get creative with your use of the chat feature to keep your audience engaged. Ask them to send a hand emoji if they can relate to something, or ask what they want to see first in your presentation.

11 Record Your Presentation

The best way to improve your Zoom presentation skills is to learn from your past mistakes. Thankfully, Zoom lets you record your presentations so you can revisit them later and analyze your performance. Are you using too many hand gestures? Are you walking around too much? Are you speaking at a reasonable pace? Understanding how you did can help you do even better in the future. You can also send your Zoom presentation recordings to a friend or family member so they can review it for you. It always helps to get the opinion of someone you trust.

**

CHAPTER 12

SUMMARY–SPEECH WRITING AND PRESENTATION

I realise that there is a lot to take in when reading a book like this. In the main, the book has been about face-to-face presentations based on traditional speech writing techniques. The previous chapter dealt briefly with remote presentations.

This is very much a beginner's guide and contains the fundamentals. The books mentioned in the useful information section go into speech writing and presentation in much more depth. However, the danger is that by pitching yourself at too high a level to begin with you will get lost in the subject matter.

However, it doesn't matter which book you read, the same underlying principles apply.

Right at the outset, I emphasised that the very first thing to consider when accepting an invitation to speak is:

■ What is the nature of the function in question and also what or who are the audience in question? Pretty obvious really but a fundamental point and one that requires some examination. What is it that you should be trying to say?

■ Following this you can then set objectives for your self that will form the basis of your speech.

Make sure that you are prepared. Do your homework and be on top of the situation. Listen to speakers, particularly good speakers and learn what you can about the art and craft of making a speech or giving a presentation.

Make sure that you have carried out thorough research around the topic of the speech or presentation that you are going to give. Knowledge is the key to everything.

When it comes to crafting a speech remember that speech writing should be a process of simplification, using language effectively to ensure that you get the most across using the minimum of words. A good speech is pieced together in a defined structure comprising the opening, introduction to the subject, the body of the speech and the close of the speech.

When you are satisfied with your speech writing skills it is then time to give some thought to your style of presentation and the aids that you might use when delivering your speech. The use of language is very important along with your posture and how you convey yourself to your audience. In addition, some thought needs to go into how you dress.

Your voice, tone of voice, is very important and plays a significant role when you are delivering a speech: the tone, the pitch, the volume and the clarity are all important elements and all can be improved with adequate training.

If you have any say in where you are making your speech it is of vital importance that you choose the right setting for your speech or presentation, the acoustics and the seating need to be right.

Of equal importance is the need to be in overall control, and to be confident that you have all the information you need concerning the event, the sponsors and knowledge of the type of audience you are to face.

Don't let nerves get the better of you, particularly if you are speaking for the first time. Carry out exercises that we mentioned in the book, try to meditate and relax, convince your self that you are in control and don't get put off by hecklers.

Finally, when you deliver your speech, believe in your self and what you are saying, know your audience and be confident. If you can get this right, you will successfully deliver the speech or presentation that you have crafted.

Good luck!

**

USEFUL WEBSITES AND PUBLICATIONS

The following websites and also publications provide a wealth of information about the art and techniques of speech writing and presentation and many also offer sample speeches for all occasions.

WEBSITES

www.dailywritingtips.com

Offers useful tips on speech and presentation writing

www.brightcarbon.com

Offers the same as above

www.theeverygirl.com

Offers tips on public speaking and presentations for women in particular but not exclusively.

www.wikihow.com/Write-a-Speech

Offers tips on speechwriting and other aspects of presentation- also offers sample speeches *https://www.skillsyouneed.com*

Offers invaluable tips on organising a speech and presentation

www.sampletemplates.com

Offers sample speech templates for presentations

https://www.myperfectwords.com/blog/speech-writing/presentation-speech

Offers good all round advice on speechmaking and presentation

**

PUBLICATIONS

Speech Writing-The Expert Guide-Simon Lancaster £12.99 Hale Expert Guides.

If after reading this book, you wish to delve deeper into the art of speech writing and presentation then the above book will be invaluable. Written by an expert in his field who has been an advisor to leading politicians and businessmen.

10 Steps to Writing a Vital Speech: The Definitive Guide to Professional Speechwriting. Fletcher Dean and David Murray. Vital Speeches of the Day (publisher)

Another excellent guide to speechwriting

The Political Speechwriter's Companion: A Guide for Writers and Speakers-Robert Lehman CQ Press

This book is geared around political speech writing and is an excellent read.

Of course, there are many more books out there all of which provide useful preparation for speechwriting and presentation.

**

Appendix 1-Public Speaking Roles and Events

Contents

1. Acting as compere
2. Acting as Master of Ceremonies
3. After-Dinner Speaking
4. Appeals and Fundraising
5. Business Meetings-Informal and Formal
6. Chairing a Meeting
7. Conference and Conventions
8. Debating
9. Funerals and Memorials
10. Key note Speaking
11. Weddings/Civil partnerships
12. Opening functions
13. Political Speeches
14. Radio and Television

Acting as Compere

Comperes are employed to link succeeding acts in a cabaret. The role of the compere, who is usually a comedian, is the public speaking role that is most closely related to performing in a show business sense.

A compere introduces the performers before they come on and will comment on their performance when they have finished with all speakers, the compere must be aware of what kind of people are in the audience and what the occasion is, and, if he knows this he should be able to make appropriate comments that draw the audience together

A compere should not treat his role as an opportunity to take over the show, or to tell his favourite jokes. Instead he will urge the audience to agree that everyone is having a good time.

The compere will always be aware of what is going on backstage, so that he can cover for hitches, problems with scenery changes, power cuts or missing performers.

The skills required are similar to those necessary for the master of ceremonies, the ability to think on ones feet and to add lib when necessary. The compere must always be aware of pacing and the mood of the audience as it changes during the evening. If you are compering, aim to keep things light hearted and to generate an intimate atmosphere without hogging the limelight.

*

Acting as Master of Ceremonies

A master of ceremonies (MC) is employed by the organizers of an event to ensure that its various stages are given some cohesion and that the event itself goes off smoothly and successfully. An MC is usually needed at formal social functions, such as a company dinner conference or courses.

An MC's duties

The MC does not organize an event and neither does he or she take the place of the chair or figurehead. The essence of the MC's job is that of liaison between all participants.

Behind the scenes the MC is (or should be) totally calm, dealing with any crisis that might arise or any last minute changes, a missing speaker, electrical problems, staff problems and so on. The MC must ensure that everyone knows what is happening when the unforeseen occurs. Guest speakers will be looking to the MC to ensure that speaking conditions are as good as they can be, and to make them feel at home. The MC should meet and greet all Speakers and ensure that their specific needs are attended to.

The public role of the MC is to act as a link between the various stages of the event. At a formal dinner, the MC will shepherd the guests into the dining area, and announce grace and toasts. At a conference, the MC will ensure that everybody is in the right place at the right time, and introduces the speakers. A good MC will make connections between one speaker and the next in much the same way as a good speaker connects each part of a speech with a linking paragraph.

The MC will ensure that the audience is not only receptive to what follows, but is also in the right mood. A lively audience may need to be quelled in order that they might be better able to take in some serious facts and figures. A subdued audience may need to be jollied up in preparation for some light-hearted entertainment. An audience whose members are likely to fall asleep after dinner will need to be woken up!

The content of an MC's speech is information. The MC must be concise and to the point, and must be sure that all of the facts that they have are right. The MC must not allow their personality to upstage other speakers.

In moments of crisis, the MC must be prepared to ad-lib, disguising any tension in the situation, and keeping the audience occupied until the event can get under way again. The skill of impromptu speaking is therefore a necessary one to acquire if you are to fill this role. The role of Master of Ceremonies is unenviable. Very few people notice when things run smoothly, everyone notices when things go wrong. The MC is a focal point for emotions when things do go wrong. The good MC will allow their own personalities to 'disappear' in the process of liaison and introduction. You will need to be a strong mature character to take on and maintain the role of MC. It is, however, an invaluable role for developing the role of public speaking.

*

After-Dinner Speaking

The majority of formal dinner occasions are hosted by organizations such as companies, clubs, associations or charities. As with many other social occasions, almost all after dinner speeches take the form of toasts and replies. In some instance, a guest speaker will also be invited, and in this case, an introduction will usually be given.

Organizing after-dinner speakers

It will normally be the role of the chairman to see that the list of toasts and speakers is drawn up, and that each speaker is introduced in the correct order. It may be undesirable for the chairman to be the person to introduce each speaker. An alternative is to employ a Master of Ceremonies to perform these functions. Whoever is in control of the proceedings, it is vital that they have a good sense of timing and also brevity. The speaker must know how to speed the proceedings if they are flagging and how to wait for the right moment before moving on.

The MC or toast-maker will ask the company to stand up while grace is said. After grace the guests sit down and the meal can begin. Whether or not you say grace, of course, depends on the nature of the guests. It may not always be appropriate.

Toasting the host

At normal functions, the host is normally an organization. It usually falls to one of the guests to propose a toast to the host. It is necessary to know something about the host, and to keep in mind the reason for the dinner. If you are not a member of the host organization, you might be able to get a copy of their annual report or some other publication that will give you some idea of what they do. You may be from a related organization, in which case you can draw comparisons between the two. Always try to mention the guests of honour if there are any. If not, the chairman or president of the host organization will count as the most important person, and you should mention him or her. Again, it is diplomatic, not to say wise, to know something about the person who will be responding to the toast, and to mention him or her in the proposing toast.

Toasting the guests

A member of the host organization is expected to propose a toast to the guests. This involves introducing the guests of honour to the company and welcoming them and all the other guests to the event. Mention guests in order of precedence, include those who have been invited because they hold particular positions or as a recognition of certain services or successes. Introduce these guests individually and elaborate on their achievements (in their official capacity). Other important guests may include titled people, prominent business people, government officials and so on. Remember to use the correct form of address when mentioning important people. After singling out individuals, next mention all the other guests. The company may be divided into groups (i.e. business groupings such as departments) so take advantage of this and find something good to say about each.

Toasting the chairman

The toast is to the head of the host organization-its chairman or president. It requires the most preparation, because it is the most individual toast. The person who is proposing the toast should most definitely know something about his career and character. Mention the personal qualities that have been of benefit to the organization, and the successful changes or projects that he or she has initiated whilst with the organization. Try to achieve balance between admiration and humour and try to avoid being over familiar or sycophantic. Avoid any subject that could be a potential embarrassment.

Civic Toasts

This toast is proposed when the civic head of a town or city is attending, such as the Mayor. It need only be a short toast to which the civic head is attending as a representative of a community and not as an individual so keep any toast politically neutral.

Toast to the ladies

This toast stands as a monument to days when women attended formal dinners as escorts to their husbands. These days, it is likely that such escorts are both male and female. If this toast is included, it is more appropriate to use it as an opportunity to thank the partners of company or club members, perhaps for their support over the last year.

Replies
Each of the above toasts requires replies which should be made immediately following the relevant toast. The purpose is to thank the proposer and make a short speech.

Reply on behalf of the guests
Once again, thank the proposer of the toast to the guests, and find something comfortable to say to him or her. The main task is to show that the guests are enjoying their evening, so be humorous if you can.

Chairman's reply
On many occasions, this is the most important speech of the evening. The chairman should use it to mention the successes of the past year and to perhaps give some idea of where the organization is going in the coming year. Avoid giving lists and make sure that you single out some members of the organization by name. It is also the chairman's job to thank the organizers of the dinner.

Introducing a guest speaker
Some organizations engage the services of a guest speaker-someone who may be connected with the organization, or who may have something of special interest to say. In most cases, a

guest speaker will be a professional engaged to amuse and keep the audience happy.

If you are asked to introduce the guest speaker, make sure that you find out who he or she is and why they have been invited. A person will always need an introduction. Even if the speaker is the President of the USA you must make an effort to connect the speaker with the event and give the audience a reason to listen. Most of all, the introducers job is to welcome the speaker and set them off on the right foot.

The guest speaker

The primary objective of an after-dinner speaker appearance is to be amusing and the major imperative is to be relevant to the occasion and topical. The brief is normally very wide-ranging and so you will need to put in some work to define the subject for your speech. You might take it from the activities of the host organization, and include scandals and goings-on in the organizations industry or sector. You might want to mention recent stories in the media. Find out as much as you can about the interests of the audience so that you can connect with their interests and concerns.

It is also useful to know something about the chairman, so that you can include a short anecdote.

The conditions in which many after dinner speakers operate are quite often difficult. The audience may, by this time, be fairly well oiled and so you may encounter hecklers or other disturbances. You may also find the audience is scattered about the room, seated at tables in groups. This means that you will have to work hard to draw audience's attention away from the events taking place in each group and to focus their attention on you. It often happens that each table may form its own little society with its own humorists and leaders. Try to pick them out early on and control their behaviour with eye contact and perhaps the occasional mention.

Vote of thanks

It is customary for a member of the host organization to thank a guest speaker on behalf of the organization. It is not necessary to summarize the whole of the foregoing speech simply to show that you, as a representative of the audience found it interesting and amusing. This is one situation in which you will need to make some notes and be ready to improvise.

If the speech has been a great success, say so, but avoid being over lavish with your praise. Even if the speech has been a total flop, do try hard to be sincere in your thanks. The vote of thanks usually ends with a call for applause.

*

Appeals and fund raising speeches

When it comes to giving away money for charity, most people are interested in the good their money might do them than the good it can do for others. No person does anything, least of all part with hard-earned cash, unless it is in some way in their interest to do so. It is not enough, therefore, to make an amusing and informative speech. Persuading people to give to charity is a skill in its own right.

When people come to hear a speech, they are fulfilling one of a number of psychological needs, as we have seen in the chapter 'Knowing Your Audience'. They are doing the same thing when they decide to give to charity. These needs in relation to charity are:

- Economic-the need to be financially better off or secure
- Physical comfort-the need to be warm, fed and healthy
- Psychological-the need to be free from worry and any form of psychological anxiety, including guilt
- Acceptance-the need to feel that other people accept them as part of a social group
- As a fund raiser-your most powerful weapon is to show in a subtle way that by making a donation, one of these needs will be fulfilled. You will find this easy or more difficult, depending on what your charity is. If it is an industry benevolent society, you will have an easier ride proving to members of that industry that one day they may need to call upon its services.

Examples are - building a children's hospital in a country ravaged by war-the emphasis is on psychological needs. 'Many of us here tonight have children of our own. They are the most precious things in our lives, and we find ourselves worried to distraction when they fall sick. In this country we are privileged enough to be able to afford health care but……'and so on.

A local charity-emphasis on acceptance needs. 'This charity is blessed with a number of tireless volunteers who are able to devote much of their spare time to it. Many of you, I know, are not able to do this-we have families to look after, and demanding jobs. However, we can all make a contribution in money, if not in time...' and so on.

The speech must be centred around the topic in hand and directly related to emotional needs.

Do not be afraid in being up front and asking for money. That is what the function is for, that is why people have attended. They expect to be asked for money. They are there because they want to fulfil one their psychological needs.

Make use of eye contact to show people that you are speaking to each individual-you have identified everyone of them and no one is getting away without paying up.

This is one speech that you read without a script. You must transmit your heartfelt emotion, and reading from a script is the surest way to fail. Convey enthusiasm, warmth and sincerity, aim to persuade and inspire.

*

Business meetings-formal and informal

The vast majority of meetings take place within the context of business. They are part of the internal and external communications process that is so important to any company. Business meetings are either formal or informal. The only real difference between the two is of context-the skills required are the same. To perform well, you need to need to be capable of persuading and able to speak coherently at a moment's notice.

Preparation for business meetings

Most formal business meetings are heralded well in advance. You should be told the purpose of the meeting and who is going to be present, and why. If you do not have an agenda, you need to ask the following questions:

- When and where is the meeting to be held?
- What is the purpose of the meeting?
- Who will be present and what is their status?
- Have the other participants be briefed with the necessary information?
- Why are you being asked to attend?
- How long is the meeting expected to go on for?

A meeting could have a number of purposes: problem solving, decision-making, selling (ideas as well as products) or transmitting information. Work out which you will be expected to do and plan your contribution accordingly.

Knowing who the other participants are will enable you to build up a picture of their needs and interests, which you will have to take into account. This is most likely to be a mixed group, at least in terms of the corporate hierarchy. Understanding what these different concerns are will enable you to speak more effectively and, if necessary, be more persuasive.

Do not aim your speech at one group only. It may be tempting to level your arguments at your superiors, on the assumption that they are the people with the power to improve your career prospects. However, this will not only irritate your peer colleagues and subordinates, it is also likely to be detrimental to your cause.

In order to have proposals of any sort accepted, you will need to have them agreed by all the people they affect. Therefore, consider all members of your audience as equals.

It is important that you know how much the other participants know about the business in hand. If they know very little, you may have to spend time presenting information before you can move on to a discussion of the issues. If they have been fully briefed you will waste time going over old ground. If it seems that there is information that participants should have in advance, suggest to the meeting organizer that it is circulated.

When you know who the other participants are, and you have found out their concerns and the information they already have, you should be able to start making assumptions about their attitude towards the subject in hand:

■ Will there be a consensus of opinion on the subject?

■ Who will be against and why?

■ Who can you count on as allies to agree with you and support you?

Finding out why you have been asked to attend is vital. You may be expected to speak on behalf of your department, or to advise because you have specific expertise. You may be expected to report on the progress of your project, or to explain problems or make recommendations. Remember to formulate a statement of your own objectives with the other participants in mind, and when you have finished preparing your contribution, check that you have addressed as many of the concerns of others as you can.

The art of persuading

It could be that the objective of your speech is to persuade-to sell an idea or other products to participants. Here are a few tips on persuasion:

■ Understand the other parties stand point: gain their sympathy by showing that you understand

■ Establish a need: you cannot reach a solution if the other party does not agree that there is a problem

■ Give suggestions and explain their advantages: relate your solution/idea to the needs of the other party, interpret exactly how it will change their life/ working conditions/ effectiveness

- Gloss over areas of minor disagreement: do not let them get in the way of the major issue; broad agreement is better than no agreement
- Emphasize areas of agreement
- Encourage a conclusion: define it and allow the other party to agree without losing face.
- Avoid coercion and the hard sell
- Show that you are committed and enthusiastic about your idea/product/solution.

Discussion in meetings

Discussion is common to almost all meetings. Participants will air their views and thrash out solutions to problems. Discussion is vital to the communications process but unfocussed discussion is a waste of time and money.

A discussion is like a speech except that it is made not by one speaker but by several. Efficient discussion relies on the participants being well informed and able to put their points coherently and concisely. You performance in discussion is just as important as your ability to make a prepared presentation.

Points to remember for discussion:

- Be prepared: read the agenda and other information. Make notes on points you would like to raise.
- Listen attentively to the other speakers. Try to identify their viewpoint. If you can, test your assumptions by asking questions. Make notes.

- Your body language should convey that you are alert and open to new ideas.
- Never whisper while another person is speaking and don't interrupt.
- Show that you value other people's ideas and that you value their point of view
- If a person has already made the point that you wanted to make, say that you agree with him or her and perhaps add your own view.
- If you are introducing a new line of reasoning or a new idea, make sure that you relate it to the subject under discussion, in the same way that you would link two stages in a speech

In general, it is the chair's role to direct the discussion and to make regular summaries to keep the meeting moving forward. If this does not happen, it might fall to you to do this.

Meetings cost time and money and each participant is being paid to attend and they are all putting aside their work to do so. Each person has to do his or her bit to ensure that the meeting runs efficiently. A good public speaker is invaluable within this context.

*

Chairing a meeting

This particular form of public speaking requires special qualities in the person who chooses to accept it. Most important of all is the ability to listen when you really want to speak.

Whatever the type of the meeting, whether formal in a context where the services of a chairman are required by law, or informal, such as departmental meetings, it is essential that the chairman remains impartial and devotes his or her energy to guiding the meeting, controlling speakers and ensuring an outcome. The chairman should never comment on the substances of speeches being put to the meeting, either for or against.

Make sure that both sides get a good hearing. You will soon be able to pick out the strong personalities among those attending, and to control them, whilst at the same time giving those who are not confident their say. You may wish to invoke the rule that a person cannot speak on any given subject or motion. If you find this useful, state this rule at the beginning of the meeting.

The only time it is legitimate for the chair to show which side he or she is on is when a casting vote is needed. If you cannot be impartial-perhaps you have a special interest in the matter in hand-you should consider delegating the chair to someone else or not accept it in the first place

Conducting business

The aim of all meetings is to get through as much business as possible. You must be able to chair effectively and continually bring people back to the point. One way of doing this is to set a time limit on each speech at the start of the meeting and be firm when that limit has been reached. Always aim to move on quickly whilst at the same time aiming not to cut people off mid-stream. This requires a certain skill and it is one that is gained by practice.

Formal meetings

Formal meetings-AGM's for example-are governed by law and the rules of the company or corporation. It is essential that the person chairing a meeting understands these laws and rules and regulations.

The first responsibility of the chairman is to ensure that the proper notice of a meeting is given, according to the body's regulations. There must be enough people in attendance to be able to conduct business. The chairman will welcome those attending and state the purpose of the meeting. He or she may also read through an agenda. The chair will then call on the secretary to read the minutes of the previous meeting and when this is complete ask whether the minutes represent an accurate record of the previous meeting and whether there are matters arising.

Finally, the business of the meeting can get under way. When the meeting is finished, the chairman will announce the date and time of the next meeting and declare the meeting closed.

Informal meetings

The vast majority of meetings are informal. They may be meetings between a client and a supplier firm, or between members of different departments. Informal meetings are not bound by the same rigid rules that guide formal meetings, but the chair still needs to be in command, and still needs the same respect in order to see fair play and to see that things are done.

As with formal meetings, it is the chairman's business to ensure that the right people attend, and that all the relevant information is circulated beforehand if necessary. During the meeting, the chairman should guide the discussion and summarize when necessary and bring matters to a conclusion. After the meeting, he or she should also circulate notes of the meeting, with details of the action agreed upon.

Although the meeting is informal, the chair still has to command respect and guide the meeting to its logical conclusion without undue personal involvement.

The role of a Chairman is a very important role indeed, requires certain skills and to be able to chair effectively is the mark of an effective public speaker.

*

Conferences and conventions

Speaking to a conference or convention is similar to lecturing. The main difference is that the audience is likely to be made up of knowledgeable people. This will mean that your speech will have to be crafted so that it is interesting and not stultifying.

The kind of speech that you make at a conference will obviously depend on the type of conference and the purpose of the gathering. Obviously, if you are going to give a speech at a conference then you will need to find out all the details that you can.

You may be there to sell your product or idea to people in your industry. You must, in this case, bring to bear all your persuasive skills. Alternatively, you may have been invited to pass on information, so you should aim to do just that. Use visual aids if you think that they will help increase understanding.

Keeping the audience interested

If you are speaking on the first day of the conference, there will usually be a capacity audience full of intent listeners. However, there is also the fact that you may be booked to speak at less advantageous times, after lunch, when people fell sleepy or early in the morning when some might have hangovers and so on. At these times, the audience will be less than attentive. Check the time when you are supposed to speak and work harder to enthuse your audience if you are booked to speak at one of these aforementioned times.

Using your time

When you are not speaking, use your time to listen to other speakers. This is not only polite but will also benefit you in that you can pick up crucial tips. You can also gauge your audience and tailor your own speech beforehand. When no speeches are scheduled, socialize with other delegates. This way, you can continue doing your homework.

Convention and conferences-Compiling a checklist

Research and prepare your conference speech as you would any other full-length presentation. Some important points to remember are:

- Have you written and delivered material for the chairperson to use when introducing you?
- Have you double-checked the details of when and where you are expected to make your appearance?
- Have you checked that you have your notes and visual aids with you?
- Have you checked personal arrangements such as hotel accommodation, travel, fees and expenses?
- Have you checked the conditions at the venue?

ON the day:

- Check that your visual aids are in position and that all necessary equipment is working

- Check the venue. Make sure that the air conditioning is working to your advantage
- Ask a steward to shepherd the audience into a compact group at the front and centre of the room, so that it is easier to make contact with them and mould their group responses
- Clear the room of odds and ends left by other speakers- paper cups, used flip charts, anything that will distract attention.

For both speakers and audience alike, conferences and conventions can be enjoyable events. They are invaluable for communicating to other members of the profession. You should capitalize on this opportunity to raise awareness of your work, product or thinking and to learn from other speakers.

*

Debating

Competitive debating

In competitive debating two teams, usually of three people each, are pitted against each other, under the guidance of a chairperson. A judge awards marks to each member of the team, reaching a decision as to which team has put forward the best argument. A motion is drawn up, for example – 'This house believes that all cars should be banned from the roads'. One team is asked to speak for the motion, the other against.

Starting with the first speaker for the motion, each team member takes a turn in this order: first speaker against; second speaker for, and so on. The aim is for each team to try to refute the arguments of the other and to establish their own arguments. In this scheme, each team member has a specific job to do, within a certain time limit.

*

Funerals and memorials

Probably the most difficult speaking occasion you will encounter is that of the funeral. This is because you will have cope with your own grief and also that of others. You will also be voicing the deepest emotions of those around you.

Funerals and memorials may be slightly different. A funeral service is normally more personal and immediate than a memorial, because the grief is still fresh in peoples minds and the people attending are likely to be relatives and close friends. A memorial may take place on the anniversary of a person's death and may include people who perhaps were not so close.

Funerals

At a funeral, the most important people are the immediate family. Find out what they would like you to say and comply with their requests. Keep your speech short and simple, personal and sincere and convey the essence of the character of the deceased. Do not over-dramatize or declaim.

The structure of a funeral speech

- Introduce the occasion. Direct the formal address to the close family, using their Christian names if appropriate.
- Describe the deceased, mentioning some good times or endearing qualities; perhaps he or she was a pillar of the community and it might be appropriate to mention status and achievements.

- Address sympathy to the family and pledge your support.
- Sum up with a few choice words, for example, the deceased was much loved, is greatly missed and so on.

Never speak ill of the dead, even if you cannot find a decent thing to say about a person and you have a personal grievance. If it is a problem, you should refuse to speak.

Do not allow yourself to be so overcome with emotion that you break down. Never drink before your speech.

In Memoriam

A memorial is likely to be less overwhelming than a funeral. It is more of a celebration of a dead person's life and work, but it is still a solemn occasion. The structure above may be adapted to a memorial by adding more anecdotes, which may be even more humorous. Try to strike a balance between portraying the private and public person, and remember to elaborate your relationship with the deceased.

*

Keynote speaking

People of high standing usually company chairmen, politicians and celebrities, are sometimes invited to deliver keynote speeches at the opening of events such as conferences, trade exhibitions and the like. The speech that they give encapsulates the essence and the aim of the event, hence the name.

Preparing a keynote speech

If you are asked to give a keynote speech, find out as much as you can about the event. If it is a conference or lecture series, find out who the speakers are and what they will be covering. Perhaps it is a sales conference. In this case, find out what products are being presented. If it is a trade fair, research the industry and find out what will be going on at the fair. You will be able to get this information from the organizers. They will also be able to tell you if there is any one aspect or theme that they would like you to cover.

- Find out who the event is aimed at: a small group of company salespeople? Members of a particular industry or the general public?
- Formulate a statement of the purpose of the event: to pass on information as in a sales conference? To promote international business relations?
- Start by welcoming everyone to the event, and thanking the organizers for inviting you to deliver the keynote speech. Tell the audience the main theme of the event

and give your thoughts. Tell them what the aims of the event are, and why they are important.

■ In conclusion, you may like to wish all participants success in their endeavours, and encouraged everyone to enjoy the event.

When you have drafted your speech, look over it to check that you have the kind of speech you have been asked to deliver-a keynote speech. Remove everything that is not closely related to the event, and ensure that you have provided some food for thought and set the tone for the rest of the proceedings. Most of all, check that what you will have to say will focus the minds of the participants on the business in hand.

*

Weddings/Civil partnerships

For many people, weddings or civil partnerships are the only time in their lives where they will be asked to give a speech. Wedding /civil partnership speeches are most often given by novices who suffer from nerves and self-doubt. However, this is one of the most important days in the life of newly weds and it is crucial that you make a good speech.

The form

Below we will be covering conventional heterosexual weddings. Civil partnership and same-sex marriage speeches should be crafted according to the occasion and the protocol that applies. However, all of the same principles of delivering a speech apply.

In heterosexual weddings, it is usual to have three speeches, and all are toasts. The first toast is proposed by the bride's father, or a close family friend or relative. He or she proposes the health of bride and groom. Next, the groom replies, and proposes a toast to the bridesmaids. Finally, the best man replies on behalf of the bridesmaids. As with all things, time has changed and the usual customs and women are now beginning to assert themselves and make a speech after the groom has finished. Also, best men are also joined by best women.

Each of these speeches need to be prepared in advance and delivered as one would deliver any speech. The following are suggestions for each speech.

The bride and groom

The toast to the bride and groom should express happiness at the occasion and wish them both luck in their new life. It is customary to compliment the bride on her appearance and to compliment the groom on his luck. You may wish to add an anecdote from having known the bride so long, or you may have a funny story about the first time you met the groom. Finish by asking the guests to raise their glasses and drink to health of the bride and groom.

The things not to do at a wedding speech

- Never make jokes about the bride or mother in law. This is pathetic and outdated.
- Never make remarks that are in bad taste.
- Avoid smut, innuendo or references to past partners
- Don't use the opportunity to score points
- Keep in mind that this is the bride and grooms special day, so only add to their pleasure.

The Bridesmaids

Next up is the groom, who thanks the proposer of the previous toast and in turn proposes the toast to the bridesmaids. The groom usually compliments the bride on her appearance and thanks her for consenting to marry him. He usually compliments on his good fortune on having found her. He thanks his best man for supporting him and for working so hard to ensure that the day has run so smoothly. Sometimes, the groom also thanks the bride's family for allowing him the honour of marrying her. However, this is increasingly seen as sexist and outdated. The groom, however, should at least thank the bride's family for accepting him in their home.

The groom then proceeds to tell a few anecdotes before he turns to the subject of the bridesmaids. He should compliment them on how well turned out they are and thank them for attending his wife so well. He will finish by proposing a toast to the bridesmaids.

The main event
The best mans speech is usually the highlight of the wedding. The audience is expected to laugh and the speech is usually timed at between five to ten minutes.
Start by thanking the groom on behalf of the bridesmaids. Add your compliments to both them and the bride.

The usual course of events after this is to say something about your relationship with the groom, and to recount some lively stories about your youth together. If you did not know each other when you were younger then tell a few stories about recent events. While it is expected that you will embarrass the groom slightly, it is important that you do not overstep the mark and ruin his reputation.

Best man's humour
You should not allow your speech to turn into a string of jokes, just for the sake of getting laughs. Never make jokes in bad taste

and keep in mind the age and profile of those present. Avoid lewd comments. At the end of your speech, read any telegrams or other communications of good wishes, and introduce any special guests. Keep this section short, as the audience might become restless.

Other speeches

If the bride and groom take a decision to vary this format, they should tell everyone involved and work out who is going to propose which toast.

If the bride wishes to make a speech, she usually takes the opportunity to propose the toast to the people who have make the wedding such a special occasion.

While you are quite at liberty to arrange for as many speeches as you wish, avoid allowing them to go on for too long. It is highly likely that alcohol, food, endless speeches and so on, will have taken their toll.

*

Opening functions

There are many different types of functions that you might be asked to either open or give an opening speech. Fetes and bazaars, shopping centres and so on. Whatever the occasion, and whatever the reason that you have been asked to speak, the main aim is always to keep it brief. On most occasions, it is likely that the audience will have a great deal to distract their attention. Therefore, four or five minutes is long enough.

Being heard

It is usually the case that you will be speaking outdoors or addressing people scattered across a wide area. You will probably need to use some form of public address system. Whatever equipment you use, make sure that you check it out before intended use.

Being seen

At a lot of functions of this kind, you may find that you are surrounded by people who are all standing. It may be difficult for people to see you. In this case, ask the organizers to give you something to stand on. Ensure that people do not crowd too close around you making it difficult for you to be seen and heard. On the other hand, you may find that the audience is scattered across a wide area with huge gaps between the different groups. In this case, ask the stewards to round people up.

149

Background research

You will need to research the nature of the occasion. It may be a charity or business. Whatever, you will need to have a good idea of the aims and objectives of the organization promoting the event.

Content of speech

Start by thanking the introducer and those who have invited you. If you have a special interest in the project or charity, you should say so.

You may need to talk about the project and the people who have made it possible, or to mention the beneficiary charity. The point is to give reasons why the event is taking place. You should say why the charity / project is a good idea and mention those who will benefit.

If you are opening an exhibition, say something about the exhibit and the exhibitors. If you are opening a trade fair, you might say something about the companies that are attending and some of the changes taking place in the industry as a whole. In winding up your speech, encourage people to take part in the function: to part with their money for a good cause; to enjoy the attractions and to look around the building. Finally, wish people a successful trade fair. Then you should declare the function open.

*

Political Speeches

More often than not, senior politicians employ speechwriters who are experienced when producing speeches for public consumption. At all levels, political campaigns are co-ordinated by professionals to present a unified front to the public.

Political objectives

The public will judge a politician by his or her promises and evidence of ability to fulfil such promises. In a political campaign each party tries to establish its political priorities as those of the country or region as a whole and to show that its candidates are honest enough to represent the will of the people and smart enough to make decisions on behalf of the country as a whole. At the same time, each party will try, by fair means or foul, to undermine in the eyes of the public the policies and candidates of the other.

You are therefore in the business of persuading the audience that you will act in their best interest and that the other candidate will not. You must defend yourself against the attacks that the other party makes against your policies and attack those of the other party yourself. You must also provide the audience with memorable phrases so that they associate you with a particular action or issue and, with a bit of luck, remember your name when the time comes to vote.

Know the audience

The most important tenet to keep in mind when putting together a political speech at any level is that the audience wants something from you. In this case they come with not only genuine subconscious needs, but with specific political issues in mind.

Each speech in a campaign is different, because at each venue the audience is different. Find out what the issues are that are most likely to be concerning the audience. Find out how members of the audience lead their lives and what the issues are. They may be mainly middle-income executives whose priorities may be good trading conditions for local business and improved schooling for their children. They may be miners or car workers. You may be confronted with an audience of students or shopkeepers. Speak to your audience about the issues that are most important to them, in language that they understand. No one wants to be represented by a person who has no grasp on their own brand of reality.

Shield-work

If you are in the business to attack your opponent, you will need to defend yourself against incoming fire. There are two things to remember here. First, never use the negative terms of your opponents. If you have been called a liar, it would do more damage than good to retaliate in the same mode.

Second, do not avoid uncomfortable issues or attacks. Deal with them immediately and get them out of the way. Aim to spend as much time as possible in your speech on the positive issues without ignoring or glossing over the negative.

Sound-bites

In these days of media campaigning, it is vital that your message is media friendly. Give your audience a memorable message and the press something to use in their headlines. The skill comes down to the words you use and the way in which you string them together. If you can use a well-tuned and catchy phrase that appeals to the public's imagination, the press will use it, and this can only be to your advantage.

Find famous quotations that you can manipulate. Most of all, find ways of saying things that are vivid and evocative.

On the platform

Political speechmaking is not for the faint-hearted. You are quite likely to be heckled in the time-honoured fashion and you will probably face hostile questioners. Learn to respond quickly and decisively. Hesitation can be construed as a sign of uncertainty. Though preparation can see you through most of the fray, only practice and a cool head can ensure that you emerge without a scratch.

*

Radio and Television

Radio and Television require the speaker to master particular skills in order to be able to transmit the right message.

Different requirements

Radio broadcasts put you across as a disembodied voice. The way you look is immaterial, and this could work as an advantage to some people. On the other hand, you will need to pay special attention to the way your voice sounds, and because your listeners cannot see illustrative hand movements, you must work harder to paint evocative pictures with your words.

By contrast, television not only allows the viewers to see you, it also has the disadvantage of amplifying the defects. You must therefore work hard at presenting an acceptable image while still making sure that what you say still makes sense and is heard above the visual distraction.

Preparation

Just as you would when anticipating an interview with a print journalist, it is essential to ask questions when you are invited to take part in a radio or television broadcast:

- What is the program?
- What is the issue under discussion?
- Why are you being asked to take part?

- What is the editorial policy of the program (is there any bias in their reporting or treatment of the subject in hand)?
- Who, if any, are the other interviewers? Contact them and find out what their views are.
- What is the program's target audience, and what is their interest in your story?
- What kinds of questions will be asked?
- Is the program to broadcast live?

Define for yourself a number of points that you would like to make. Write down these points and think of a way that you could illustrate each one. You should be able to make each of your points in short concise sentences.

Try to find out, if you can, what kind of introduction you will be given. Check the facts and correct them if you know them to be untrue or biased. Find out what the first question is going to be-knowing the first question should at least give you some comfort at the outset when your nerves are bound to be on edge.

In the studio

When you enter the studio for the first time, you are bound to be slightly bewildered by all the paraphernalia. You should just ignore it. Listen carefully to instructions and try to stay relaxed. If you can, have a look around the studio before you go on air.

Voice control for radio

When answering questions on radio, speak at normal volume, as if you were having a conversation. Take care to breath normally. If you are nervous you may become breathless, make every effort to control this. Because you can't be seen, you can use a cue card or crib sheet. Make every effort to avoid rustling papers.

Body language for television

Good television technique comes with experience. But the home video camera now provides a useful way to practice before your actual performance. If you have the time and resources, record your rehearsals and compare your appearance and mannerisms with those people that you see on television every night.

Get used to making yourself comfortable in a hot seat. Ensure that your body is balanced but you are so relaxed as to be slouched in the deepest recess. Put your hands in your lap and leave them there. Keep them away from your head and face at all costs and do not fiddle.

Never look at the camera, keep your eyes on the interviewer and talk only to him or her. Make your face expressive-this is where the camera will be concentrating-but not too expressive. Concentration can often show on the face as a frown, which can be interpreted as anger.

Nerves can also be transformed into a fixed smile, which can be interpreted that you have something to hide or that you are being flippant about a subject that you should be taking seriously.

Avoid moving too much, without looking as if rigor mortis has set in. If you make sudden large movements, the camera operator will have great difficulty keeping you in shot, and the effects can be quite startling.

Speaking beyond the interviewer

For both television and radio it is quite important to remember that you are speaking to an audience of millions rather than to a single person. The presence of a studio audience should help, but make sure that you remember the need to explain yourself to others rather than take it for granted that the audience knows what you mean because the interviewer does.

Answering questions

The basic rule for answering questions for television or radio broadcasting are the same as for other question and answer session: listen carefully to the question, and answer it in a few words. Avoid plain yes or no answers, but keep your answers to a couple of sentences for the sake of time.

It may appear that given the direction the questions are taking, you will not get a chance to state your key points. If this is the case, you may need to take control of the interview. Don't be rude or stubborn-answer the questions put to you quickly and then go on to re-orientate the interview in the direction you want.

Nobody likes to see interviewees refuse to answer questions. If there is a subject that you do not want brought up on air, tell the interviewer or researcher beforehand. Get agreement that the subject will not be touched upon.

Speaking on radio or television does not always take the form of the arranged interview or panel discussion. You may be stopped in the street and asked to give your opinions on a particular subject, or you may be asked to comment over the telephone on an event or issue. You may call in to a phone-in, goaded into airing your views by being forced to listen to those of others.

However you may become involved, the broadcast media are such powerful means of mass communication that it would be foolish for anyone who regularly speaks in public to overlook them.

**

www.straightforwardco.co.uk

All titles, listed below, in the Straightforward Guides Series can be purchased online, using credit card or other forms of payment by going to www.straightfowardco.co.uk A discount of 25% per title is offered with online purchases.

Law

A Straightforward Guide to:

Consumer Rights

Bankruptcy Insolvency and the Law

Employment Law

Public law

Business law

Family law

Small Claims in the County Court

Contract law

Intellectual Property and the law

Mental Health and The Law in the UK

The Rights of Disabled people

The Rights of Disabled Children

Divorce and the law

Leaseholders Rights

Knowing Your Rights and Using the Courts

Producing your own Will

Bailiffs and the law

Being a Litigant in Person

Probate and the Law

Company law

What to Expect When You Go to Court

Give me Your Money-Guide to Effective Debt Collection

Property

Letting Property for Profit

Buying, Selling and Renting Out property

Buying a Home in England and France

Housing Rights

The Process of Conveyancing

Private Tenants Rights

Crime Reference

The Crime Writers Casebook

Being a Detective

A Comprehensive Guide to Burglary and Robbery

A Comprehensive Guide to Arrest and Detention

A Comprehensive Guide to Drink and Disorder

Creative Writing

A Straightforward Guide to:

Creative Writing

Freelance Writing

Writing your own Life Story

Writing performance Poetry

Writing Romantic Fiction

General

Creating a Successful Commercial Website

Bookkeeping and Accounts for Small Business

Buying and Selling Online

Buying and Selling Property at Auction

The Straightforward Business Plan

The Straightforward C.V.

Successful Public Speaking

Handling Bereavement

Individual and Personal Finance

Tax and Small Business

Go to:

www.straightforwardco.co.uk